D0368643

FROM ORGANIZATIONAL DECLINE
TO ORGANIZATIONAL RENEWAL

Recent Titles from Quorum Books

The Investment Side of Corporate Cash Management
Robert T. March

A Practical Approach to International Operations
Michael Gendron

Exceptional Entrepreneurial Women: Strategies for Success
Russel R. Taylor

Collective Bargaining and Impasse Resolution in the Public Sector
David A. Dilts and William J. Walsh

New Directions in MIS Management: A Guide for the 1990s
Robert J. Thierauf

The Labor Lawyer's Guide to the Rights and Responsibilities of Employee
Whistleblowers
Stephen M. Kohn and Michael D. Kohn

Strategic Organization Planning: Downsizing for Survival
David C. Dougherty

Joint Venture Partner Selection: Strategies for Developed Countries
J. Michael Geringer

Sustainable Corporate Growth: A Model and Management Planning Tool
John J. Clark, Thomas C. Chiang, and Gerard T. Olson

Competitive Freedom Versus National Security Regulation
Manley Rutherford Irwin

Labor Law and Business Change: Theoretical and Transactional Perspectives
Samuel Estreicher and Daniel G. Collins, editors

The Constitutional Right to a Speedy and Fair Criminal Trial
Warren Freedman

Entrepreneurial Systems for the 1990s: Their Creation,
Structure, and Management
John E. Tropman and Gersh Morningstar

FROM ORGANIZATIONAL DECLINE *TO* ORGANIZATIONAL RENEWAL _____

THE PHOENIX SYNDROME

Mary E. Guy

QUORUM BOOKS
New York • Westport, Connecticut • London

658.4063
G98f

Library of Congress Cataloging-in-Publication Data

Guy, Mary E. (Mary Ellen)
  From organizational decline to organizational renewal : the
phoenix syndrome / Mary E. Guy.
    p. cm.
  Bibliography: p.
  Includes index.
  ISBN 0-89930-372-2 (lib. bdg. : alk. paper)
  1. Corporate turnarounds. 2. Organizational change. I. Title.
HD58.8.G89 1989
  658.4'063—dc19   88-18706

British Library Cataloguing in Publication Data is available.

Copyright © 1989 by Mary E. Guy

All rights reserved. No portion of this book may be
reproduced, by any process or technique, without the
express written consent of the publisher.

Library of Congress Catalog Card Number: 88-18706
ISBN: 0-89930-372-2

First published in 1989 by Quorum Books

Greenwood Press, Inc.
88 Post Road West, Westport, Connecticut 06881

Printed in the United States of America

The paper used in this book complies with the
Permanent Paper Standard issued by the National
Information Standards Organization (Z39.48-1984).

10 9 8 7 6 5 4 3 2 1

To J. Wayne Campbell,
without whose thoughts on the matter
this book would never have materialized.

University Libraries
Carnegie Mellon University
Pittsburgh, Pennsylvania 15213

Contents

Figures and Tables

Cases in Point

Preface

PHOENIX: A legendary bird represented by ancient Egyptians as living five or six centuries, being consumed in fire by its own act, and rising in youthful freshness from its own ashes.

Lunching with a colleague some time ago, we began talking about various organizations we have known that resurrected themselves from almost certain demise. We recalled the path of their declines. Most of the examples from both the public and private sectors were characterized on the downside by declining productivity, deteriorating service, high personnel turnover, and an internal climate of secrecy and mistrust.

On the upside, there was a characteristic nose-to-the-grindstone ethos with a well-defined goal of resurrecting the organization. As our discussion continued, we realized the obvious: Decline-followed-by-renewal is not an unusual occurrence. This book sets forth examples of what I call the Phoenix Syndrome—organizational decline to a point just short of total failure, followed by renewal or "rising from the ashes." How much of this phenomenon is a natural part of the normal life cycles of organizations and how much is rational, willed, and planned varies from case to case, but the point is that it happens. This book unveils and explores this process.

The purpose of this book is to move beyond impatience with decline and its corollaries and develop organizational theory so that it acknowledges the enduring characteristics of organizations in decline as well as in renewal. I argue that upon objective analysis, there are conditions and circumstances under which it is understandable—even acceptable and justifiable—to allow, plan, orchestrate, and manage the decline of an organization. Market demands, political realities, hidden agendas, strategic planning requirements, and many other factors influence such behavior. I hope to convince readers, though, that it is a challenging task to reduce an organization to a "heart death" state without also incurring "brain death." To manage decline and subsequently resurrect an organization requires expert managerial skill, perception, and control. The late Supreme Court Justice William O. Douglas' warning to be ever vigilant of oppression applies as well to being alert for organizational decline: ". . . there is a twilight when everything remains seemingly unchanged. And it is in such twilight that we all must be most aware of change in the air—however slight—lest we become unwitting victims of the darkness" (Douglas, 1987, p. 162).

Ideally an organization is able to function with such vitality and resilience that it can withstand the rigors that crises and a turbulent environment bring. In reality organizations move from one level of organizational health and resilience to another as they are bombarded with stresses from their internal and external environments. By familiarity with the stages of the model described in this book, readers should be able to pinpoint where their organizations are positioned and gain insight into what is likely to follow.

Chapters 1 through 6 trace the pattern of events within declining organizations and then contrast these with the pattern of events in organizations going through the renewal process. Vignettes are provided from both public and private organizations to illustrate the topics under discussion. Chapter 7 presents an example of an organization in the midst of the Phoenix Syndrome and shows how the syndrome, as a theoretical model, is useful for studying an organization over time. It presents the case of the National Aeronautics and Space Administration. The explosion of the Space Shuttle Challenger on January 28, 1986, brought to a climax the predicament of an organization incapable of successfully identifying its decline and doing something about it before a major disaster occurred. The loss of the orbiter and its crew of seven, including the first public school teacher to fly in space, was experienced as a national catastrophe. The success of the Shuttle program had become a powerful symbol of America's excellence in space. The disaster and the investigations that ensued drove NASA deeper into decline as the public became more aware of the managerial shortcomings which had beset the agency many months and even years prior to the tragic launch. Chapter 7 traces the agency's progress through the stages of renewal and speculates on its future.

The Phoenix Syndrome, not unlike the Peter Principle, Parkinson's Law, Murphy's Law, and Janis' groupthink phenomenon, bespeaks the obvious as well as the subtle. It is my hope that this book, which presents a model of decline-followed-by-renewal, will open the door to fuller appreciation and discussion of the characteristics and pattern of events accompanying the processes of decline and renewal.

Acknowledgments

Having spent all my working life enmeshed in formal organizations, I am fascinated with them. Each organization is a human creation, structured to achieve human ends, but each organization becomes more than a sum of its parts. It takes on a momentum and life of its own, and the people of the organization treat it as a creature unto itself. Much as an anthropologist would conduct a participant/observer study, I take pleasure in standing back from my participation in the daily business and in watching what happens. Life in organizations is a fascinating spectator sport.

This book is an exploration of organizational decline and renewal that I have derived from my own experiences and observations as well as from those of many others. For all my experiences that yield insight into the process of decline-followed-by-renewal, I am grateful. I must acknowledge J. Wayne Campbell, for it was over lunch that he and I started swapping stories of decline and subsequent resurrection in organizations we both had known. I thank him for his experiences, insight, and interest in the phenomenon we have come to call the Phoenix Syndrome.

Three students of organizations, Vee Stalker, Harris Cornett, and Cecil Usher, have provided insights and cases which exemplify various stages of the Phoenix Syndrome. To them, my teachers disguised as my students, I say thank you.

I am grateful to a young organization on the rise, Errand Express, Inc., and its CEO, Cindy Michelson, for not only embellishing my experiences but lending me the microcomputer for processing all the words you are about to read. If and when decline gains a toehold in

Errand Express, Inc., may the resurrection come swiftly and successfully.

I had the pleasure of benefitting from superb research assistants as I wrote this book. David H. Coursey will probably now tell you that he has done more sleuthing into organizational decline and renewal than he ever imagined he would. He has been invaluable during this project, and I wish him great success in his own career. Lynne Windham has also been very valuable in helping me put the finishing touches to this work. She has courageously pricked my conscience to remove sexist expressions and metaphors. Without the technical assistance of another graduate student, Norma Ann Dodd, this manuscript would have taken far longer to produce than it did.

Finally, I must thank Blaine Brownell, Dean of the School of Social and Behavioral Sciences, and David W. Sink, Chair of the Department of Political Science and Public Affairs, at the University of Alabama at Birmingham. They have provided me with the luxury of time and support while I completed this project. To the University of Alabama at Birmingham, I also say thank you for being yet another data base.

PART I

THE DOWNSIDE OF THE PHOENIX SYNDROME

1

Benchmarks of Decline

Most people interested enough in organizations to look at them closely do not look at organizations in decline. They look at those on the rise and hope to learn from success. This bias toward optimism is typical in all facets of American life. When it comes to sports everyone applauds the winners not the losers. It is part of the American character to be more concerned about what makes us progress and do well than what makes us slump and not do well. The truth of the matter is that progress and decline are opposite sides of the same coin.

So what is decline? Just as progress is a process, so is decline. It is a journey, not a destination. Decline is most apparent when organizational effort repeatedly fails to yield success. In other words, decline is a prolonged suboptimization of productivity. Although suboptimization of productivity may occur in any organization at a given point in time, the stamina of the organization is determined by the presence of countervailing forces and forward movement. In the absence of these, suboptimization degenerates into a downward trend difficult to thwart. If the organization continually fails to meet its goals, the decline may end in the total failure of the organization. Decline is only possible where sufficient resources exist to avoid instantaneous collapse. Conceptually, only firms with adequate slack resources have the luxury of tolerating a decline. Those without reserves of credit, cash, and personnel do not go into a decline. They simply fail.

Decline of an organization may be subtle or obvious. It may be sudden, with a precipitous fall in revenue, public image, or internal stability. On the other hand, it may be barely noticeable, evolving slowly, imperceptibly, over the years. Decline may be unintentional on the part of management, or intentional. It may be passively allowed when it could be prevented, or it may be actively (though usually covertly) supported.

Oftentimes the well-meaning management team will encounter symptoms of decline but not recognize them as harbingers of decline. The whole is obscured by attention to isolated events and a failure to analyze the broader implications. For example, the early warning signs listed below name isolated events that are noticeable individually but may not be recognized collectively as symptomatic of organizational decline. Since decline is a process, it is difficult to identify when or how it starts. In hindsight, both economic and subjective deterioration may have been obvious. Phenomena which may signal decline are

- consistently poor opportunity/cost choices
- absence of long-range planning (or any planning)
- resource allocations in the absence of a dialogue about priorities
- finance-related organizational weaknesses
- short-term cutbacks (deferrals) and organizational nearsightedness
- decreasing profits
- organizational turmoil
- pervasive employee discontent
- increased absenteeism among employees
- unusually high personnel turnover rate
- insufficient information traveling through the formal communication channels of the company, producing suspicions throughout the organization that leadership is withholding information
- the grapevine among staff buzzing louder than usual
- negative coverage in the media

Organizations are either progressing, maintaining, or declining. Short-term, periodic decline is often unavoidable and may be inevitable, even in the best run companies. It may even be healthy in the life cycle of an organization. Stated another way, growth and decline patterns are to be expected in the life cycles of organizations. But this is why decline is often not dealt with in its early stage. As management makes a decision to wait out the situation at hand, hoping things will get better, it assumes the decline is only temporary. Sometimes this is the case, but sometimes decline is a trend and events go from bad to worse.

ECONOMIC VERSUS SUBJECTIVE DECLINE

There are usually several benchmarks that clearly herald decline. Those that relate to resources or profits are economic. Those that relate

Table 1
Economic and Subjective Benchmarks of Decline

Economic	Subjective
• declining sales	• loss of prestige or reputation
• declining market share	• pessimistic tinge to corporate culture
• declining profits	• negativistic climate among staff
• financial loss	• perception that firm is in decline
• declining resources	• service level inadequacy
	• unclear priorities
	• loss of leadership, direction, or goals

to how people perceive the well-being of the organization are subjective. As shown in Table 1, economic benchmarks include declining sales; declining market share; declining profits; financial loss; or, especially in public organizations, declining resources. Subjective benchmarks include a loss of prestige or reputation; a pessimistic tinge to the organizational character; a negativistic climate among staff; a perception among employees and consumers that the organization is in decline; service level inadequacy; unclear priorities; and loss of leadership, direction, and/or goals.

By the time the benchmarks fit together as pieces of a puzzle, the bulk of the damage has been done. This is not to say that the damage is irreparable, but overcoming inertia to reverse the trend from decline to renewal requires extraordinary measures. The unfortunate aspect of these economic and subjective benchmarks is that they are not, in and of themselves, the cause of decline. They are merely indicators of decline, just as their opposites are indicators of success. Additionally, it is debatable whether any one economic factor is a cause of a subjective measure or vice versa. There are circumstances in which there is no relation between economic factors and subjective perceptions. While people perceive the firm to be succeeding, its financial health may be failing; or, while a firm is doing well financially, people perceive it to be in trouble and withdraw their support, thus producing economic problems. Such a combination of economic and subjective factors works to speed decline. The story of Tampa General Hospital demonstrates this interplay.

CASE IN POINT: TAMPA GENERAL HOSPITAL

In the past few years, many hospitals have found themselves in decline. This includes those that are public or nonprofit as well as those that are investor-owned. With the public tightening its belt when it comes to paying for health care, hospitals have had difficulty avoiding revenue shortages. In the early 1980's Tampa General Hospital, in Tampa, Florida, reflected the plight of many other public hospitals caught in a changing healthcare environment (Fanning & Wiley, 1984). Patients who had insurance or could afford a higher level care than that provided under public funding moved to "for-profit" suburban hospitals. This left Tampa General with a high volume of medically indigent patients who could not pay their bills. Its profit margin decreased each time it lost a paying patient, and the money problems of the hospital became public knowledge. Paying patients who otherwise would have continued going to the hospital stayed away as they perceived it to be less desirable than others in the community.

Comments in the media about Tampa General and public general hospitals like it gave this sort of description: "struggling to stay alive," "losing the competition (with private hospitals)," and "hospital of last resort." These pessimistic phrases had a debilitating effect on management and staff, adversely affecting attitudes and motivation. The financial pinch led to painful consequences such as layoffs, work overloads, excessive debt, and postponing new equipment purchases. There was a decline in services, sometimes to the extent that patients were turned away. The hospital's reputation in the community suffered. Staff and equipment shortages led physicians and other health care professionals to emigrate to private hospitals. And the decline spiraled deeper.

Economic benchmarks of decline assume different configurations depending on whether the organization is private or public. In the business sector declining sales, declining market share, financial losses, either a sudden or gradual downturn in revenues, and declining profits all signal decline. In most public agencies, sales, market share, and profits are meaningless terms. Instead, a decrease, or failure to receive an increase, in annual allocations signals a decline.

Subjective benchmarks may occur in conjunction with economic benchmarks or may appear independently. An organization may be in decline as a result of perceptions, regardless of financial reality. Service-level inadequacy provides an example. A public agency, with its relatively fixed level of resources, may appear to be in decline simply because it cannot provide all the services demanded. In private businesses, expectations of consumers may change faster than a company's resources. When this happens the organization gives the appearance of being in decline because it cannot meet the changing expectations of the marketplace quickly enough. In a worst case scenario this service level inadequacy can amount to operational bankruptcy.

Clientele of an organization may perceive it to be in decline when it is actually functioning normally. This is especially the case when citizens complain about government agencies. Public agencies are often criticized for being organizations without the capacity to sufficiently satisfy demands. Constant-rationing theory explains this perceived state of decline—which is actually not decline at all. It is simply the state of the art for redistributive government policies. Public organizations, especially taxing jurisdictions such as cities, are in a constant-rationing situation. This can best be described by the following analogy. If gasoline rationing is imposed and a driver goes to a service station to buy five gallons of gasoline, that person may only be allowed to purchase two gallons. The driver is unhappy with this but takes the two gallons, pays for them, and drives away, satisfied that everyone is treated the same. At least there is some perceived equity because the driver only had to pay for the two gallons received. However, in a local government context citizens pay their bill (taxes) up front. They are "entitled" in their opinion to all of any government service provided as well as some of which are not provided. Therefore, when they request a service from government and do not get it, they, in their perception of the situation, have been wronged. They were "entitled" to the service because they had already paid for it. The problem is that for many practical and political reasons, government cannot provide all of any service that members of a diverse electorate demand. This makes the government service context more complex than rationing, but at least puts government in a constant-rationing situation. It is apparent that government will never be able to meet the expectations of all citizens, and when perceived equity is absent, clients are dissatisfied.

Rationing is a form of organizational satisficing in which the agency does the best it can to provide a modicum of services for the public with the dollars it has been allocated. This should not be misinterpreted as decline. Decline is a downward spiraling, in which the organization does enough to survive, but not enough to stop the devolution.

Decline is not unique to the public and nonprofit sectors. Although it may be gratifying to think that private businesses have no resources to waste on allowing decline to continue, in fact, private firms frequently decline because

- All decline is not recognized as decline.
- Tax write-offs available from inherently inefficient organizational operations are a good justification for businesses to tolerate, even foster, declining activities.
- Private companies, no less than public ones, need managerial "elephant graveyards" into which substandard, near-retirement, "Peter Principle" employees can be tucked away. These Phoenix Syndrome units are periodically revived when changes in the profit picture, newly discovered opportunities, or a sagging market position in other corporate functions, require their rejuvenation. Such a resurrection is designed to bolster the parent organization's efforts, earnings, tax position, or productivity.
- Strategic planning may show that some activities, while marginally useful in the present, will not be necessary until ten to fifteen years hence. In these cases, the units in question may be allowed to sink to a low ebb to be "reborn" later. Revival or rebirth may be necessary even when organizational death is initially planned if there is a flaw in the strategic planning process, or if market priorities change.

Just as subjective benchmarks herald the decline of public general hospitals, they also foretell of problems in other types of organizations. Johnson & Johnson, the makers of Tylenol, are fully aware of the thin line between a crisis and decline and the role subjective judgment plays in contributing to decline. When its popular over-the-counter analgesic, Tylenol, was tampered with, it moved quickly to isolate the event and regain the public's confidence in the safety of its products. Had Johnson & Johnson not moved as quickly as it did, and as decisively, the crisis would have evolved into a decline.

CASE IN POINT: THE TYLENOL SCARE AS CRISIS BUT NOT DECLINE

Johnson & Johnson, along with its subsidiary, McNeil Consumer Products, had to work hard and fast to recover the market share it lost because of public distrust of Tylenol. After a series of tampering incidents in which cyanide had been added to Tylenol capsules, Johnson & Johnson announced it was discontinuing capsules and switching to caplets (Molotsky, 1986). The manufacturers contended that it is more difficult to tamper with caplets than capsules. The decision represented an attempt to reassure the public of Johnson & Johnson's concern for consumer safety and to symbolize its concern for product safety. This was a successful strategy and as a result Johnson & Johnson emerged from the crisis with its market share intact and successfully forestalled decline.

In comparison to the constructive actions of Johnson & Johnson, the South Carolina Department of Mental Health failed to act aggressively to quell criticism of the way it conducted its business. In a public agency subjective benchmarks of decline may culminate in a public outcry of dissatisfaction, followed by an audit commissioned by the funding agency.

CASE IN POINT: SOUTH CAROLINA DEPARTMENT OF MENTAL HEALTH

In South Carolina, public dissatisfaction with the policies and procedures of the South Carolina Department of Mental Health (SCDMH) resulted in the State Legislature mandating an audit of the agency. Conducted by South Carolina's Legislative Audit Council, the final report cited a series of problems in management: failure to properly investigate and act on patient abuse claims, misuse of state property by employees, inadequate planning, unnecessary capital expenditures, and inadequate training for paraprofessionals (Legislative Audit Council, 1983). This audit would never have been conducted if there had not been the perception by the public that there were serious problems in the Department.

Organizational culture and climate are indicators of subjective measures of decline. Although subjective decline, when ignored, runs the risk of becoming economic decline, proactive measures can isolate an impending crisis and prevent decline. For example, organizational development efforts were used by AT&T when cultural changes were imperative for it to meet the challenges of divestiture and a competitive environment.

CASE IN POINT: AMERICAN TELEPHONE & TELEGRAPH

Following divestiture, American Telephone & Telegraph has headed off decline by maintaining a steady information flow among employees, keeping them abreast of changes and, at the same time, warning that a new day has arrived. The corporation issued a special commemorative edition of *Bell Telephone Magazine* heralding changes and urging employees to maintain loyalty to the company but become entrepreneurial in spirit (Tunstall, 1983). AT&T employees had suddenly found themselves working in a competitive environment in which the public could go elsewhere for service if it was dissatisfied with AT&T's service. The organizational development activities were designed to modify employees' attitudes and prevent decline from setting in.

Individuals' perceptions and the perspectives from which they view circumstances largely determine their judgment of an organization. Subjective and objective measures interact with one another to accentuate service level inadequacies and unclear priorities. In summary, subjective measures, as well as objective measures, must be brought into any equation of organizational vitality and resilience.

DEALING WITH DECLINE

A variety of behaviors accompany the realization of decline, ranging from denial to blaming others to actually working on a turnaround. A classic example of denial is that practiced by the South Carolina Department of Mental Health following its censure by the Legislative Audit Council report. Rather than deal with the problems identified, groupthink (Janis, 1982) took over and blame was placed on the committee that conducted the audit. There was an attempt to kill the messenger, rather than attend to the message. The South Carolina Department of Mental Health, in order to head off public censure resulting from the critical report, contracted with a private firm to conduct a management audit of its own, paid for by the agency. This action demonstrates an organization clearly caught in a cycle of decline that had yet to be acknowledged. But decline cannot be rectified until it is recognized and addressed. A reaction of anger, finger pointing, and explaining the problems away consumed time and energy that would have been more effectively spent addressing and correcting the problems.

Other unproductive reactions are opposite to the denial practiced at the South Carolina Department of Mental Health. For example, demoralized agencies sometimes adopt a reaction of acquiescence, futility, giving up, and giving in. Another route is to blame the situation on external causes beyond the control of the organization. Still another is to concoct an enemy within or outside the organization and blame it for the woes, focusing energy on this common enemy.

Another response is to reorganize and change key staff, hoping that reshuffling the deck will make the next hand better. One of the standard practices at many companies when problems start is to "shake up" the firm by reorganizing and shifting people around. Often this does more damage than leaving things the way they are, because it breaks up what few work groups are working well together, and speeds up the development of suspicion, low employee morale, and high turnover. Changing the management team without uncovering the root cause of the problem is a case of jumping to conclusions and inadequately exploring alternatives before taking action.

It is not unusual for decline to occur in a tiered fashion, with one level or segment of the organization moving inexorably downward and the rest of the organization remaining oblivious to the fact. Even when told about the predicament of the level in trouble, problems are denied because they have not yet been felt in other parts of the organization. The pockets of darkness are overshadowed by the successes in the pockets of light.

There may be some correlation between the stages of reaction by cancer patients to the knowledge of their condition and the stages of reaction by managers upon discovery of decline within their organizations. The patient must first recognize the disease. Through recognizing the potential of the disease, the patient can come to admit, rather than deny, the symptoms and garner the desire to overcome the disease. Similarly, this is the pattern for combatting a declination trend:

1. recognizing the decline
2. admitting the decline
3. developing a strategy to overcome the trend
4. implementing the strategy
5. monitoring success of the strategy and making adjustments when necessary to maintain a steadily progressive course

Decline itself is an unpleasant issue. Although indices such as market share, quarterly profits, turnover figures, production costs, client satisfaction, and budgetary allocations are monitored, problems are usually addressed in segments. This segmentation frames any discussion of decline as resulting from isolated events and avoids the overall acknowledgment that decline has gained a foothold in the organization. Only among the closest of friends do managers give voice to their concerns about a disease besetting the company. This is especially true when they feel responsible for not having identified the problem earlier.

As well as the overall issue of decline, smaller, circumscribed issues become undiscussable when things are not going well. As the organization becomes more insecure, so do the people within it. Turmoil results from an overactive grapevine, with staff trying to second guess what is happening. Resources are allocated without a clear dialogue on priorities. Financial strain on the budget mounts. The organization becomes near-sighted, overreacting to small problems with little regard for long range planning. It deals with superficial issues rather than overriding problems. Organizational entropy takes over, in that when left to themselves, things go from bad to worse. Employees become discontented and find fault with management even when they have been formerly satisfied with the same behaviors.

CASE IN POINT: UNEMPLOYMENT CLAIMS OFFICE

The manager of a citywide unemployment compensation claims office found himself in the midst of a discrimination suit after the agency had gone through a series of employee cutbacks and overall budget cuts. In May, 1983, he was presented with a suit filed by seven black employees alleging racial discrimination. He admitted, in hindsight, that the grapevine had been buzzing but he had been oblivious to it. He had prided himself on dealing fairly with minority employees, going out of his way to promote them whenever possible. He cited several events that contributed to the deterioration of relationships between him and his subordinates. His blindness to what was going on was probably more a function of his not looking clearly at the organization as a whole, in the context of the cuts it had undergone. In other words, he had failed to deal with the decline itself and was unaware of employee discontent. He was so accustomed to seeing himself as a "bleeding heart liberal" and had been called guilty of reverse discrimination enough times that he had not considered the possibility he would be displeasing minority employees.

In the nine years preceding the lawsuit, the Birmingham Claims Office had been reduced from sixty-seven employees to only sixteen. Rumors at the time of the lawsuit were that the office would be paperless in the not too distant future, with only five or six employees needed. The Reagan Administration's description of unemployment compensation as "vacation pay for freeloaders" did nothing but increasingly depress the already low morale of the office. People felt threatened. The next job classification lost could be their own. The threat of being laid off and not knowing what would happen next engendered suspicion to the point of paranoia. For example, the list of complaints against the manager included (1) two employees felt the manager was checking on them when he called to wish them speedy recovery while they were on sick leave; (2) three employees reported they were reprimanded for taking excessive break time and felt this was unreasonable; and (3) two employees reported they were discriminated against because they were denied annual leave because of pressing work demands. Four of the seven plaintiffs were at the lowest rank in the office. Should any more positions be eliminated, they felt it would most likely be theirs (Cornett, 1984). After the trial *(Wilson, Jr. v. State of Alabama,* 1985), the judge ruled in favor of Cornett, the manager, declaring that the workload and Cornett's attempts to serve the public with as little delay as possible were accountable for the plaintiffs' complaints. The scenario painted by Cornett is common to organizations in decline. When the going gets tough, management "battens down the hatches," and retreats to offices away from most of the employees. When employees are cut off from communication, they batten down their own hatches, and suspicions multiply.

Government agencies, although they can certainly decline, are rarely reduced to ashes. Rather, the culmination of their decline is usually an absorption into another agency. Freeman (1982) has studied patterns of public organizations. He says:

> Because local government units seldom actually disband, reorganization is probably as close as we can come to a comparable phenomenon. For Chicago, Detroit, and Philadelphia, departments and sections of city government were studied over a period of 85 years. Yearly rates of formation and dissolution for divisions ranged from 6 to 10 percent, and for sections of divisions, from 13 to 24 percent. (p. 6)

The fact that the Unemployment Claims Office employees' jobs would be salvaged in one form or another was insufficient to diminish the threat they assumed they were facing.

Consistently poor opportunity/cost choices and the absence of long-range planning coincide with decline. Planning tends to be short term and focuses on superficial problems. Rapid change is tried with little attention to the unintended consequences which follow. Persecutory thinking occurs, with management looking around for targets to which their fingers can point.

DECLINE AS PART OF THE LIFE CYCLE

It is the rare firm that does not go through a cyclical pattern of declines and resurrections. In younger organizations, the cycles are compressed and easier to pull out of because there is a lack of tradition and it is easier to see decline early in the process. Decline in young firms is usually the result of too little revenue to provide the promised product. As the organization ages, it develops means for coping with such financial stress. Thus decline in older firms is not as identifiable in its early stages. Decline in a mature organization may be a result of dysfunctional traditions, customs, or habits that once were functional and contributed to the organizational mission. Such subtle causes of decline take much more time to develop, identify, and rectify.

CASE IN POINT: COOPER GREEN HOSPITAL

A chronology of Cooper Green Hospital in Birmingham, Alabama, since its inception in 1888 shows the following pattern (Stalker, 1984). Created in 1888 as the Hospital of the United Charities, it met its first significant decline in 1892 when it was beset by personnel and financial problems. Community support rallied in 1895 and with adequate funding, personnel problems subsided. In 1904 community support was withdrawn, leaving the hospital in dire straits. The year 1912 brought a restoration of funding. In 1922 there were allegations of inadequate care and an investigation ensued. By 1932 a new advisory board had been named and the hospital was on a smooth course until 1953. In that year there were charges of substandard care. Problems persisted, but the hospital kept its doors open amidst controversy about funding and quality-of-care standards. In 1965 the county provided a relatively stable indigent care fund from which the hospital could draw. By 1983 the community was again paying attention to the hospital, with complaints that the money had not been managed well. In 1987 the hospital was in the throes of a community debate about whether to increase its funding or close its doors. The stages of decline and resurrection demonstrate that the cycle between resurrection and decline lengthens as the firm matures. As an organization grows more financially secure, it has more slack resources and can afford to decline more before it comes close to the point of ashes and must be resurrected or self-destruct.

Stages in the Life Cycle of Cooper Green Hospital

Decline	Resurrection
1892	1895
1904	1912
1922	1932
1953	1965
1983	?

This pattern is not unique to the public sector. It also happens in private organizations. The difference is that there is often no funding source to maintain struggling private firms with their financial burden. They are forced to close or convince venture capitalists to believe in them long enough to show a profit.

CASE IN POINT: FEDERAL EXPRESS

Federal Express is a private sector firm that went from crisis to crisis for the first several years of its existence, only to rise as a Phoenix into a darling of Wall Street (Sigafoos, 1983). It is predictable that it will reach another decline, and the challenge will be to see if it can rise dramatically again. Fred Smith started Federal Express in 1972 with a little money and a lot of optimism. By 1974 the company had serious cash flow problems and by March of that year had a financial loss of $5.5 million. Although he had some narrow escapes, he turned the losses around and showed a net income of $3.6 million by 1976. By 1983 Federal Express showed a total revenue of over $1 billion with a net income of almost $89 million.

Several factors seem to make the difference between decline and excellence: management expertise, leadership, technological advances, clear goals with the means to achieve them, and an accurate reading of the environment.

Management expertise. When intentionally withheld, the organization risks declining. When the management team is skilled and its decisions focus on the well-being of the organization over individual self-interest, the organization is one step closer to excellence.

Leadership. When present, the organization is closer to excellence; when withheld, the organization is inviting troubles. The cohesiveness necessary for the employees as a whole to work toward a common goal dissolves.

Technological advances. When ignored, the firm is denied the competitive edge, thus leading to its status as a second class citizen. When present, the firm holds a competitive edge.

Regular, meaningful reevaluation of the link between the organization's goals and the procedures for meeting them. When this is a tradition, potential decline is headed off before too much damage occurs. When it is not done, organizations persist in preset patterns, even when meeting their objectives no longer achieves the goals of the firm: Management continues the same traditions because they worked in the past.

An accurate reading of the environment. When the demands, opportunities, and challenges confronting the organization and its products are acknowledged, administrative decision makers can take advantage of what is about to come. When the environment is misread, challenges are not foreseen and opportunities are missed. Given the rapid changes in modern society, the stakes are high, and it is perilous to ignore or misinterpret changes on the horizon.

SUMMARY

This chapter presents an overview of organizational decline.

• The declination trend is a downward spiraling of the firm. The deeper it is in the process of decline, the more indicators, or benchmarks, there are of decline.

• Perceived decline is contrasted with real decline. Although observers—either within or outside the firm—may perceive the firm to be declining, it may actually not be. For example, government agencies routinely delivering services are often cited as being in decline as a result of consumers' expectations of equity. On the other hand, the agency may be in real decline if indicators of decline are present, such as lowered resource allocations, staff unrest, and marked public criticism. Decline is a state of mind as well as a financial fact. An organization may be perceived to be in decline even when its financial picture looks rosy.

• Decline, or the threat of decline, is a commonly encountered phenomenon in the life cycle of an organization. In some cases it can be avoided; in some it cannot. In some cases managers actually support the decline; in others they constructively battle it.

• Perhaps the greatest hurdle for management is to acknowledge decline when it occurs, rather than overlook it or try to affix blame for it on someone or something outside the organization.

2

Types of Decline

This chapter discusses the functions of decline, demonstrating its useful aspects as well as its pathological side. When used to solve a short-term problem, suboptimization is a strategy that temporarily reallocates or conserves resources. When prolonged, with no end in sight, suboptimization is a euphemism for decline. It literally means doing less than best. In a culture in which a firmly held value is that bigger is better, suboptimization sounds antithetical to "good" management. But there are times when suboptimization is a rational managerial action. For example, when a budget is too short and funds are running out, there must be a plan for suboptimizing in order to continue providing necessary services. This requires a rationing of resources under such strictures that services decline to a minimally acceptable level—just to get by. Work slowdowns are another example of a suboptimization strategy. Certain sets of employees, primarily those not allowed to engage in collective bargaining, will determine the minimally acceptable productivity that will be tolerated. They then orchestrate a decline to achieve their ends. This is a suboptimization strategy—a means of doing less than the best in order to achieve a goal.

Rational suboptimization strategies are means by which particular goals may be reached: to await the beginning of a new fiscal year with the organization still viable, to achieve demands of labor groups, to reallocate available resources, or to buy time while new markets or products are developed. Whetten (1980) points out that some organizations have to make themselves smaller in order to be able to produce sufficient profits and survive. Downsizing, such as that practiced at CBS, is an intentional, short-term strategy to reallocate resources.

CASE IN POINT: CBS DOWNSIZES

CBS announced on July 1, 1986, that it would undergo a "painful" paring of personnel. As many as 600 people were on the layoff list. A team of executives had analyzed the financial status of CBS and recommended this strategy because profits had declined and advertising revenues were not growing enough to maintain the level of operations of mid-1986 (Associated Press, 1986c). Reductions in force of this type occur periodically as an organization adapts itself to the changing demands of its environment.

Internal to the organization, suboptimization strategies are practiced by management when resources are removed from one organizational unit and reallocated to another. It is not unusual for one unit within a company to fail to contribute to the mission of the organization as successfully as the other units. When management's goal is to maximize achievement of the organization's mission, it is practical to remove resources from the unit failing to contribute to the effort and reallocate to those units which do. This strategy results in a decline of the deviant unit but makes room for an optimizing strategy in other units. In a discussion of organizational life cycles and natural selection processes, John Freeman (1982) describes a case which exemplifies a rational suboptimization strategy designed to result ultimately in an optimization of mission. Speaking of semiconductor manufacturers, he cites the following: "As the inventory of devices developed and the market expanded, firms found that the research and development effort required to be first was often inconsistent with the allocation of effort to produce efficiency" (p. 12). The firms with "first mover advantage" in a niche tended to edge out competitors, making the competition's previously expended research and development effort in that niche a waste. In an effort to cut their losses but appear to the stockholders and the industry in general to continue to be aggressive, firms can allow the decline of research and development. This enables them to subsequently buy a niche-dominating competitor as a means of regaining a market foothold. This is a constructive use of decline, not mismanagement as it would appear to those working in research and development.

Occasionally such reallocation strategies ultimately result in an almost total metamorphosis of the firm, the final result of which may be newly found health or organizational death. Again, Freeman speaks on this. Metamorphosis models ". . . suggest that as organizations grow, they change so dramatically and discontinuously that it might be useful to view the later version as an example of a different form" (p. 13). But

Freeman warns that marked change may sound the death knell of a firm. "This is to say that one of the ways in which failure occurs is through metamorphic change. . . . [It] may be the last, desperate act of a failing organization. Such acts of desperation are as likely to bring on the end sooner as they are to stave it off" (p. 13).

However, the organization may metamorphose into a form which can compete better in a different niche and be managed more effectively. Planned decline in one niche, only to revive later in another is an example of successfully using decline to move the firm forward. The decision model used to orchestrate this decline-followed-by-renewal is one that represents choosing a means which will retard growth. Intentionally orchestrating decline to bring forth a more vibrant firm is a rational suboptimization strategy.

A suboptimization strategy used successfully in the public sector is that of cutting services, or at least threatening to, in order to cause a clamor among current or potential clientele. This strategy mobilizes latent interest groups who target legislators and lobby for higher allocations. For example, Peters (1980) describes what happened when in 1975 President Ford planned to cut Amtrak's budget. Amtrak announced that with the proposed cut it would have to delete a number of routes. The routes to be discontinued just happened to pass through the states of the Chair of the Senate Commerce Committee, Senate majority whip, and Senate majority leader, among others. It came as no surprise, then, to learn that a majority of the Congress voted to maintain Amtrak's budget.

DIAGNOSTIC CATEGORIES

Decline may be categorized into three types: undiscovered, uncontrolled, and orchestrated. These types of decline are not mutually exclusive. The differentiation is that each type is driven more by one attribute than by another. In fact, decline may start as orchestrated and become uncontrolled, or it may move from undiscovered to uncontrolled.

Within each category intentionality and rationality help to clarify the function of the decline. Figure 1 depicts these three types of decline, along with their respective possibilities for being intentional or unintentional, and rational or irrational. Only when decline is intentional is it relevant to consider the rationality of it. If it is intentional, it may or may not be rational.

UNDISCOVERED DECLINE

Undiscovered decline occurs when the indicators of decline are present but those in control of the firm do not recognize them as signals

Figure 1
Types of Decline

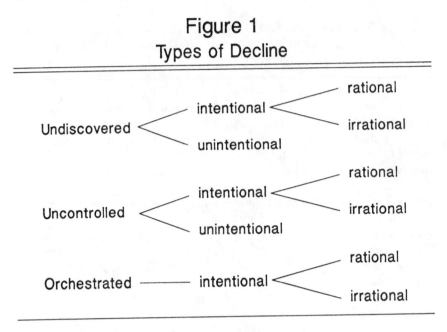

of decline. This lack of awareness may occur as a collective denial mechanism, or it may be that the signs or symptoms have been noticed but no one yet recognizes the decline as substantive. When undiscovered decline is intentional, it is put in place by some actor or set of actors functioning outside the awareness of others in the organization. Intentional, undiscovered decline is a variant of orchestrated decline and may be rational or irrational, according to the criteria by which rationality is judged.

Several well known companies provide examples of undiscovered decline. Just two years after Peters and Waterman's book, *In Search of Excellence*, reported on forty-three "excellent" companies, *Business Week* reported that at least fourteen of them had lost their luster and were in decline (1984a). The cover story suggested that twelve of the fourteen stumbling firms had failed to adapt to fundamental changes in their markets and had gone into decline that remained undiscovered for a prolonged length of time. The fourteen faltering companies listed were Atari, Avon Products, Caterpillar Tractor, Chesebrough-Pond's, Delta Air Lines, Digital Equipment, Disney Productions, Eastman Kodak, Fluor, Hewlett-Packard, Levi Strauss, Revlon, Tupperware, and Texas Instruments. Each of these companies had failed to identify its decline and act on it until it had become blatantly obvious. Walt Disney Productions presents an excellent example of unintentional, undiscovered decline that continued until management finally acknowledged the problems and instituted major changes.

CASE IN POINT: DISNEYLAND

At Disneyland, Walt Disney was successful in creating and maintaining an organizational climate in which all employees felt a responsibility to maintain a friendly, clean atmosphere at the amusement park. Emphasizing the importance of the individual employee in maintaining an organization's image, employee applicants are screened for just the right attitudes (Branst, 1984). *In Search of Excellence* cites Disney for this ability to maintain a clearly focused corporate culture among the work force. But active, positive employee participation has not been enough to prevent decline. Disney fell by the wayside because of its inability or unwillingness to read the market. At Disney, television revenues dwindled from $44.4 million in 1982 to $27.9 million in 1983. The theme parks in California and Florida had virtually no increase in attendance from 1973 to 1983. The parks were still the company's core business, bringing in 87 percent of Disney's income in 1983. In his statement exemplifying undiscovered decline, the CEO at that time, Ronald W. Miller, said "It was clear that we were in never-never land. Yet we wouldn't let ourselves go" (*Business Week*, 1984c, p. 50). Since that time a new CEO, Michael D. Eisner was hired and has been credited with turning Disney around by vitalizing its movie productions.

Miller's lament of undiscovered decline is not unusual for that of an organization in decline. In hindsight those guiding the firm were able to see they had maintained a course charted long age, one that no longer led down a guaranteed path to success. The benchmarks of decline were clearly present but not interpreted as such: Long-range planning was absent and sales were declining, Disney had lost some of its previous market share, and it had lost the luster of its former prestige. Ironically, Disney was already in a declination trend when Peters and Waterman wrote *In Search of Excellence*, but the decline had not yet been discovered—not by those in the company, and not by those outside the company.

UNCONTROLLED DECLINE

Uncontrolled decline exists when a firm is spiraling downward, people are aware of it, and yet the resources necessary to stop the process and turn it around are unavailable. Discovered but uncontrolled decline may actually be uncontrollable decline. Intentional, uncontrolled decline is rational or irrational depending on the perspective taken and is another variant of orchestrated decline. If one is in agreement with the strategy and believes that the assumptions are well founded, then it is rational. On the other hand, if one disagrees with the strategy and does not believe that the tactic is well founded, then it is irrational.

For example, an intentional, rational, suboptimization strategy of uncontrolled decline was used by Chrysler Corporation. By just waiting until the decline was obvious to everyone, the corporation was successful in procuring the financial resources to stay solvent.

CASE IN POINT: CHRYSLER CORPORATION

The Chrysler Corporation's near failure did not happen overnight. The corporation declined over a period of time. By waiting until it was almost at the bottom, it was able to mobilize a plethora of interests to lobby for a public bail out, including numerous automobile-related businesses, labor, and municipal interests. Lobbying for a governmental bailout before all interests pulled together would not have produced the needed funding, given the initial opposition and controversy surrounding the proposal. The Congressional vote, when it finally did pass, was 241–124 in the House of Representatives and 43–34 in the Senate (a vote far short of overwhelming approbation).

A similar example of rational but precarious timing exists not in one organization but in a system of organizations—the U.S. public schools. The decline in the public education system has been apparent to various factions for the past decade but it was not until recently that it became so marked that interests within the profession of education were ready to take action.

CASE IN POINT: U.S. PUBLIC EDUCATION

By waiting until parents were dissatisfied, teacher training colleges were dissatisfied, teachers were dissatisfied, and students themselves were dissatisfied, the U.S. Department of Education was able to mobilize enough interest to start public education on its way back to excellence. By publicizing *A Nation at Risk* in 1983, the National Commission on Excellence in Education drew together a coalition of interests ready to tackle the problem. Remedies were outlined in *The Nation Responds* by the U.S. Department of Education (1984). This report has been followed by additional strategy documents. In 1986 the Carnegie Forum on Education and the Economy published *A Nation Prepared: Teachers for the 21st Century*. This report called for radical changes in teacher training programs as well as school administration practices. What would have been disregarded a few years earlier was now being taken seriously.

An insidious form of destructiveness in uncontrolled decline occurs when those who should be in control of the situation are careless and do not pay attention to what is happening around them. These people allow things to happen around them but do not intervene in a proactive way. They get caught in the predicament of reacting to situations rather than creating situations. Of the three sorts of people (those who watch things happen, those who make things happen, and those who wonder what happened), these are the ones who wonder what happened. These are people who, when things start falling around them, are so busy applying band-aids they fail to see the implications for the organization as a whole. While decline is actually happening around them, they fail to address it. People responsible for managing must have a broad view of their role and be able to see not only the trees but the forest. Ineptness in this role is manifested by someone who is unable to connect the actions of a department to the well-being of the organization as a whole.

Additionally, simply not caring is a human response, which can occur for any number of reasons. It is another insidious cause of decline. When the person does decide to care, it may well be too late to stop the devolution already in motion.

ORCHESTRATED DECLINE

Orchestrated decline is the most undiscussable on the continuum of organizational decline. Because orchestrated decline is obviously intentional, the interesting question is for whom is it rational? Characteristic of this kind of decline are the tactics used to cover up intentional, planned decline of the organization or of a unit within the organization. Tactics used by administrators in attempting to insure that planned decline is not discovered by client groups, the general public, elected or appointed officials, boards of directors, shareholders, immediate supervisors, or peers are

- delays in implementing improvements, e.g., a "wait" that is unclear as to purpose
- reports of false progress (one step forward, two steps back)

- protestations of innocence: "I don't control," especially where a board, committee, or commission is involved
- blanket denial (meanwhile pointing to false progress)

The demise of the War on Poverty programs provides an example of decline orchestrated more by those outside the agency than those within. Since there were no particularly clandestine efforts to kill the programs, it is a "discussable" variation of orchestrated decline.

CASE IN POINT: OEO PROGRAMS

The creation of the Office of Economic Opportunity and its mission was met by enthusiasm in the mid-1960s. By the mid-1970's, however, this enthusiasm had waned and even its early proponents were experiencing ambivalent feelings toward it. The optimistic attempts to change the status quo of poor people in the United States brought with it a burst of energy, commitment, and public resources. After years of applying OEO efforts to the problem, however, the initial burst of optimism gave way to feelings of futility among agency personnel, clientele of the agency, and the public at large. The decline in public interest reflected a pattern not orchestrated by forces in the organization. Rather, it reflected a predictable pattern of waning interest. Somewhat like being the "hula hoop" of social policy, its popularity fell. As a result, Congress and the President were unwilling to allocate substantial funds. Thus the decline of the OEO program was orchestrated by those outside the agency, whose efforts were not met by substantial resistance from those within the agency.

One of the constructive reasons for allowing decline to occur is that it can be a tool to devalue an entrenched power base in private, nonprofit, or public organizations. The person or persons in charge may be unable to be removed from their positions for political reasons. When an influential position is held by someone who is no longer taking the company line, or for some other reason is not contributing to the mission of the organization, decline can be used to unseat that person. In public agencies, this occurs with political appointees or persons with a political power base so influential that to unseat them would be to lose critical funding elsewhere. In private firms this occurs when the person(s) in charge of the miscreant unit have so much influence in other parts of the firm that to unseat them would mean losing momentum in other units. Or, for political reasons, to unseat the incumbent would be to anger necessary power bases elsewhere in the organization, in the community, or on the governing board. In voluntary organizations, any combination of these situations can exist. To unseat an ineffective but influential person may do more harm than good until it is obvious to a significant number that the person is not capable of doing the job that needs to be done. In simpler terms, this process of devaluing the entrenched power base is what is commonly known as giving the person enough rope to hang himself, instead of having to pay the unpopular price of hanging him yourself. Because secrecy is built into the process, this sort of orchestration has a negative side effect. An air of Byzantine politics soon pervades the organization. In other words, people sense that while appearing to operate in the light, management is actually operating in the shadow. People become wary of what they are told, not knowing whom to trust.

Another constructive reason for orchestrating decline is simply to accompany the life cycle of the product. A particular product line has a life cycle and so does its manufacturing process. Planning for the termination of the product's life requires planning for the demise of the organization or unit which produces it. This is a rational process which requires foresight and planning. In this sort of orchestration secrecy does not have to be built into the process.

Public opinion sometimes governs when an organization will decline. The War on Poverty of the 1960s came to an end when the American public changed its collective opinion. The public decided that the Federal Government could not afford, nor would it be successful in the attempt, to eradicate poverty. As public opinion went from optimism to pessimism, the funding for the involved agencies diminished. In times of cutbacks secrecy usually occurs. When people feel their jobs are threatened and no one is sure who is going to be laid off next, the grapevine buzzes and rumors abound. Misinformation spreads and people become increasingly anxious. It takes healthy, open communication to manage agencies that are being consistently cut back. Without it more time is spent listening to, and speculating on, the latest rumor than is spent working.

In a Machiavellian sense, orchestrating a decline can be a constructive maneuver by a board of directors to persuade those in control of an organization that change is necessary. There are times when those who ultimately must implement changes refuse to see them as necessary to spur the firm forward. This happens when the organization has been successful with its current strategy, and the management does not yet realize that what proved successful in the past will no longer produce success in the future. One strategy is to withhold resources from the organization and wait until decline is set in motion to draw management's attention to the predicament.

Another constructive reason for allowing decline to continue, even if it is not intended originally, is to bring the plight to the attention of decision makers more quickly. It will increase the probability of successfully overcoming the predicament. This is what Hurst (1984) calls a "creative stall." It is a wait that produces or perpetuates a downturn, but it is done with the foresight that a good end will come from the action. Additionally the foresight involves the recognition that good will come from the downturn faster than it would come if the organization were forced to continue to be successful.

The case of Chrysler Corporation presents an example of a creative stall. The corporation attempted to receive government backed loans prior to the Congressional vote that finally approved it, but was unsuccessful. By waiting until its bankruptcy jeopardized industries across the nation, the wealth of cities, and thousands of families, they were able to receive guaranteed loans denied them earlier when the threat to the nation's economy was not as grave. Understand that it was not good management that caused Chrysler's dilemma; it was a remarkable lack of foresight. But once the decline was in progress, then continued decline became a strategy of making the best of a bad situation.

Another example of a creative stall occurred at GEICO. John J. Byrne, Chief Executive Officer of GEICO, recounts how the company muddled through until the managerial staff was ready to accept a change (Sherman, 1983). By waiting until the time was right, Byrne was able to maintain a constructive culture and still manage a change.

> A corporate culture can be a valuable asset for a company, facilitating internal communication and providing stars to steer by. But the culture can entail costs when circumstances call for major change in operating rules or corporate goals. When conflict between the culture and the need for change arises, a wise manager will strive to keep the culture from getting badly damaged. It's not easy to repair or replace. (Sherman, p. 80)

Another constructive use of orchestrated decline occurs with setting priorities and choosing how to spend a finite amount of resources. One unit may have to be shortchanged in order to salvage another unit that is more essential to the organization as a whole. This is a rational allocation of scarce resources and represents the end result of a tough decision-making process. Many organizations encounter this when there are not enough dollars to accomplish everything that needs to be accomplished. Although those in charge of the units that are shortchanged complain that the decision is not rational, those who make the decision will declare that some decision rule had to be used and utility to the company was the one used. To the decision makers the decision is rational.

Whether orchestrated decline is constructive or destructive depends on whether the end goal of the plan is to benefit or hurt the organization. The differentiation fades when good intentions result in detrimental consequences, or when bad intentions turn into positive consequences. One of the destructive reasons for decline centers around the human passion for revenge. Seeking personal vengeance for a wrong by declining an organization is difficult to fathom for some but it occurs. Because of each wronged person's perspective, it is difficult to draw generalizations from this scenario except to say that someone can hurt someone else, or a group of others, by turning a formerly successful venture into a flop.

In conclusion, there are times when orchestrated decline is good management. American sportsmanship, upon which managerial behaviors are often based, does not value decline. It values winning. But there are situations when well planned decline benefits the organization. The challenge is to maneuver the decline so that it benefits rather than harms the organization. The difficulty of dealing with decline is that it is an unpopular topic and people are uncomfortable discussing it. There are few lessons in how to decline an organization, and few kudos await the staff who accomplishes it.

INTENTIONAL VERSUS UNINTENTIONAL

Intentionality is an important characteristic of decline. Undiscovered and uncontrolled decline may be intentional or unintentional, whereas orchestrated decline is obviously intentional. When decision makers choose to allow a firm, or a unit within the firm, to go into decline and stay in decline, then it is orchestrated and intentional.

Decline that is intentional on the part of significant organizational actors has a different flavor than when it is unintentional. The former results from a purposeful decision to suboptimize. In such a scenario, those orchestrating the decline actively work toward the development of a declination trend in the organization. Because it "makes sense" at least to some subset of decision makers, it is not only predictable and planned, but also rational. When decline is intentional, those who have the power to stop it choose not to do so. Although aware that the organization is in decline, no action is taken to stop the declination trend from building momentum. Those in control have a plan of action to orchestrate the decline and are prepared to justify their actions if confronted or "stonewall" and deny them.

Unintentional decline results from a strategy that was not purposely meant to suboptimize. It produces unpredicted, unforeseen suboptimization that does not "make sense" to the observer and was never intended to happen.

RATIONAL VERSUS IRRATIONAL

Rational and irrational acts are never far apart. Actually, they may be one and the same, depending on who is doing the evaluating. The stamp of rationality presupposes a comprehensible value schema such that the person judging the decline can understand why the organization is behaving as it does. That is, there is a logical reason for the action. Because one person's objectives may differ from another's, that which is rational to one is irrational to another.

As soon as people think that a major behavior of the firm is intentional and irrational, a strange air surrounds their conversations. Those acts that are suspiciously irrational also become undiscussable, or only discussable in whispered voices. Employees echo the caution that it is neither wise nor fruitful to question the rationality of what appears to be a clearly irrational act when it has been sanctioned by top level management. At best the behavior reflects the fact that top level decision makers know something the others do not. At worst, the behavior reflects the fact that those lower are powerless to stop the action.

People accommodate what seems to be irrational behavior. The psychological phenomenon that results, functionally designed to accommodate everyone to the strategy in question (to which the firm is committed), is consistent with cognitive dissonance and its correlates. People have a need to have consistency between their behavior and their thoughts. If it is too difficult to change the behavior, then the alternative is to change the belief. Adherence to a belief that is illogical is oftentimes stronger than adherence to that which is logical because of the psychic energy required to suppress one's doubts. For example in the 1970s American auto manufacturers insisted consumers wanted large, gas guzzling autos. As they held steadfast to their position, buyers were turning in droves to foreign car manufacturers who were making smaller, cheaper, more fuel efficient cars. Why did the American auto industry not see this? Because the industry was committed to an irrational path of behavior. The manufacturers had a choice of changing their behavior and manufacturing a different type of automobile, or maintaining faith in their traditional product regardless of the market. They chose to do the latter until confronted with losses so great they verged on financial crises. Because they had faith in their traditional product, they chose not to see the truth until long after it had become readily apparent.

Durham and Smith (1982) argue that natural selection accounts for why some organizations die and others survive. In the case of American automobile manufacturers, which have been tested severely, it has been human judgment and reliance on routines that has produced problems for them, and it has been human judgment and innovation that has saved them (Holusha, 1986). Manufacturers live and die by their ability to read the environment and understand their market.

A suboptimization strategy that appears irrational to clientele may be rational to managers, given the constraints within which they must work. For example, in crowded public health centers a triage concept for providing service is often utilized. In other words, clients for whom there is a reasonable expectation that provision of services will ameliorate their presenting condition are provided services immediately. Those for whom there is little expectation that provision of services will improve their condition are denied immediate services. This is a concept from battlefield hospitals: Given few resources, it is best to treat those for whom there is the expectation that services will make the difference between life and death. Those who will survive without services are denied them and those who will probably die even if they are treated are denied. The goal is to save as many lives as possible, and within the constraints of that goal triage is a rational suboptimization strategy.

Another example is that which accompanies the decision of which patient shall receive a donor organ. Those for whom the likelihood is slim they will live very long after the transplant are not chosen. Patients who do not need the organ to survive are not chosen. The patients selected are those for whom there is a reasonable expectation that receipt of the organ will result in prolonged life.

In the worst of cases, a managerial tactic that starts out as rational may evolve into a strategy that is irrational for most, if not all, of the organizational actors. Through the phenomenon of groupthink (Janis, 1982), which demands consensus, a failing tactic is continued because no one is willing or courageous enough to question the basic premises that underly the strategy. Long-term planning is foregone in favor of short term considerations.

CASE IN POINT: SPACE SHUTTLE'S O-RING FAILURE

On the day the Rogers Commission released its report probing the Challenger accident, one of the commission members was interviewed on the *MacNeil/Lehrer NewsHour* (1986). Dr. Richard Feynman, a Nobel Prize winning physicist, asserted that the Space Shuttle Program had many warnings that there was something wrong and that sooner or later a tragic accident would occur. Developing an analogy that likened the engineers who produced the solid rocket boosters to parents, and the management of the Solid Rocket Booster project at Marshall Space Flight Center as a child, he gave the following explanation. Just as a child will run in the road and be warned by his or her parents not to do so again because it is dangerous and the child could be hit by a car, the child will retort "But nothing happened." The child runs out in the road again, several times, and the parents keep saying that it is dangerous and harm will come. "Sooner or later the child gets run over. Is it an accident? No, it's not an accident" (p. 5). In terms of organizational decline, Feynman is saying that long-range planning in the form of repairing a faulty seal design was foregone in favor of "running out in the road again and again" daring fate. The focus on the short term, that nothing serious had happened in previous flights, blinded Space Shuttle managers to the inevitable fate of Challenger.

Those who point fingers and claim that an action is irrational may be responding subjectively. As already noted, one person's rational act is another person's absurdity. An action is judged to be irrational by the person whose goals are not being maximized. When a unit of a firm is left to wither, the action may be rational on the part of the organization as a whole, but it is irrational for the employees of the unit since their jobs and careers are at stake. First and foremost, a person's employment objectives revolve around one's self-interest regarding job security, salary, career mobility, and status.

The recent spate of industrial closings, only for them to reopen within a suspiciously short time hiring nonunion employees is irrational in terms of labor interests. To those in charge of generating profits, however, the choice is rational. When union breaking is a means for cutting costs, breaking them is in the interest of the organization and is a perfectly rational act.

A secondary objective of employment is to promote personal growth and development of personnel. But this objective is never as important to the employer as the primary objective, which is to get the work done as efficiently as possible. Organizational rationality is a question of whether a decision will be good for the company.

Sometimes irrational acts occur not as the action of any particular individual or set of individuals. Rather it can occur from structural *hysteresis*, a term coined by Jeffrey Ford (1980). By this he means that with organizations there is a lag, a hysteresis, between what is done and what should be done. For example, in its most constructive sense, hysteresis occurs in small firms that are quickly growing. The structure of the organization is developed much later than it needs to be. Dynamic, growing organizations typically do not have the luxury of planning a structure and carefully prescribing policies and procedures.

Structure and routinization come after the fact—an irrational but understandable event. On the other hand, an older, top heavy organization that needs to loosen its structure to cope with rapid change or new technology also shows this lag—in this case to the obvious detriment of the organization and its mission.

DIFFERENTIAL DIAGNOSES

It is difficult to distinguish between organizations engaged in undiscovered decline from those that are the victims of uncontrolled decline. In undiscovered decline, management simply does not see it, which may be a result of organizational inertia.

> Existing organizations derive their competitive advantages from the stability of their internal social relationships and on the basis of their relationships with other organizations. This often leads to the development of ideologies and traditions that at once legitimate the status quo and dampen innovative tendencies. (Freeman, 1982, pp. 17-18)

The struggle that characterizes the firm's creation is avoided later by reliance on established methods and established structures that are resistant to change, even when they fail to be optimally productive. In uncontrolled decline, management is in partial control even though factors in the larger environment (economy, government, or special interest groups) may be vying for input.

Periodic decline is an example of uncontrolled, unintentional decline. This type of decline is foreseeable by those both within and outside the organization. It results from an event or process that is discussable, such as predictable seasonal fluctuations of the market, hiatus near the end of a fiscal year, end of a grant period, end of product newness, or the predictable waning of market interest.

There is no such creature as an organization invulnerable to decline. The most constructive approach to it is to address the threat head-on. Caterpillar, a manufacturer of earth-moving equipment, provides an example.

CASE IN POINT: CATERPILLAR

Caterpillar represents an example of the evolution of decline from undiscovered to discovered but uncontrolled, to the beginning of organizational renewal. At Caterpillar, a firm labeled as excellent by Peters and Waterman, things went precipitously downhill. Caterpillar experienced a fall in worldwide demand for its equipment. Beginning in 1982, the decline marked an end to its forty-eight-year profit streak. To survive, the company changed its basic product strategy. Chief executive officer Lee L. Morgan said "We've reexamined ourselves to the very heart of the organization, questioning everything we do" (*Business Week*, 1984b, p. 91). Caterpillar moved away from competing with advanced, enduring machines, selling at premium prices, and offering fast service. Instead, Caterpillar cut prices and called on partners overseas to produce competitive equipment. This reexamination and change in objectives that reversed the declination trend is an example of acting decisively to stop an otherwise uncontrollable decline (Stavro, 1986).

One more example from large, formerly successful, American corporations is at John Deere, a traditional farm equipment company long respected for manufacturing a quality product. It has moved from undiscovered, unintentional decline to uncontrolled, unintentional decline.

CASE IN POINT: JOHN DEERE & COMPANY

Making an incorrect forecast, decision makers at Deere thought that as the farm business slowed down, construction would increase. They moved into manufacturing large earth-moving equipment, only to watch themselves move frighteningly close to defiling the corporate culture as well as the corporate coffers. The Deere 855, the main large piece of equipment produced, proved faulty. Deere dealers around the country were unhappy or unready to take on the responsibility to monitor and service a product they knew very little about and saw as being somewhat outside the traditional purview and interest of the company. In order to fend off further decline, Deere recognized the situation and switched back to what it knew best, and what its dealers knew best—small and medium lines of equipment (*Business Week*, 1984d). However, the farming industry declined and Deere's market for traditional farming equipment suffered. The long-term strategy to invest in an automated farm equipment manufacturing plant in Waterloo, Iowa, proved faulty. As the company passed its 150th anniversary in 1987, it had to grapple with what direction to move to regain its former vitality (Deveny, 1986).

Slow decline is more difficult to see than abrupt decline. The short-term change at John Deere is easier to identify as decline than when the decline is so gradual as to be unnoticeable. Thus, John Deere's decline should be easier to stop than that experienced by Disney, if the negative impact of the farm economy is controlled.

Sometimes what appears to be uncontrolled decline, is only a return to normalcy. For example, after a surge of business, demand may settle back to a more normal level. In retail stores the periodic rush of business in late fall each year reflects the Christmas rush. The winter months then reflect a predictable seasonal decrease in retail sales.

Still another example of predictable decline is that which results from a shift of attention to something else. This happens in public sector agencies when the news media focus on one agency long enough and forcefully enough so that a boon of resources are allocated to the agency, or a shift in management results. For example, if an unpopular Cabinet member is railed publicly long enough, and a clamor arises for a change in leadership, the person will be replaced. Following the replacement, attention is redirected away from the agency, allowing it to decline from the temporary above average momentum resulting from the massive infusion of interest.

An example of externally imposed orchestrated decline results from predictable market forces. While hospitals were thriving and increasing the number of beds on a regular basis, the desire of the market to cut hospital costs has caused a sudden turnaround. Passage of the Tax Equity and Fiscal Responsibility Act of 1982 brought with it the diagnosis related group (DRG) billing method for prospective payment of health care providers. This payment method provides a built in incentive for hospitals not to keep patients any longer than absolutely essential. This has caused a decline in hospital occupancy, with some hospitals closing altogether, most laying off staff, and all tightening belts. This is a decline due to external forces that has also caused decline among hospital supply companies (*Business Week*, 1985).

Sometimes the question of rationality/irrationality revolves around personalities, sometimes it revolves around organizational units, and sometimes it revolves around units as a function of the personalities involved. For example, there are cases in which the officer in charge has a personal vendetta for the head of a unit and will set situations up so that the unit fails, in order to emphasize the inadequacies of the person in charge.

At other times, "misfits" of an organization are assigned to a marginal unit. In this way they are isolated from the rest of the organization, still to produce at least minimally, but not to be involved in the mainstream of the organization. This unit-turned-turkey-farm may appear irrational since it is a sorry conglomeration of minimally effective performers. However, given the constraints of many employment regulations, it is often easier and more efficient to set minimal producers aside than to try to fire them.

While researching hospitals, Guy (1985) found a public hospital that used a particular unit for those staff not bad enough to fire but not good enough to be productive members of the hospital. This is an example of top management designing a unit to deal with decline as a way of sealing it off from the rest of the organization. From one vantage this is a rational strategy and from another it is irrational. It is rational when the objective is to maximize output from all employees, have at least a minimum output from the weakest employees, and foster positive camaraderie. By removing the truants from the high producers, the latter's productivity is not stymied. Because one embittered employee's grousing can have a detrimental effect on a significant number of productive employees, this avoids tainting the character of a potentially vibrant work unit by a few influential grousers. However, this strategy is irrational if the objective is to maximize each person's output. When this is the case it is better to intersperse weak employees among the strong ones. This serves to mainstream them, provide role modeling, and diminish the impact of their lower output.

The current dilemma in public education is the irrational result of what started out as a rational objective. With the social activism of the 1960's came an ideology that higher education should not be the province of the elite—rather it should be the province of everyone who wanted to attain more learning. Because of this, the open-door policy was implemented in many colleges.

The open-door policy means that students enter colleges without the traditional requisite skills to perform reading, writing, and mathematical operations. After students have passed through this educational system, many become teachers working in the public school system and passing on what little they know to upcoming students. This system has continued until recently, and the American public educational process has been steadily declining (National Commission on Excellence in Education, 1983). The crisis in education began with a laudable goal to educate everyone. But this resulted in mediocrity, with too many ill-prepared teachers producing poorly educated students (Kerchner, 1984).

Observers may argue over the rationality of waiting to the last possible moment before acting to reverse decline. Habits are a trait of human behavior: A routine will be maintained just because it has been used before. And this succinctly explains why organizations allow themselves to dwindle almost to the point of their demise. The crisis in education, the federal deficit, and the near bankruptcy of major industrial firms, have neared the precipice because of persistence in routines rather than because of a rational timing strategy. Even when behavior is unproductive, the actor is more likely to maintain it than to attempt to change.

The federal deficit provides an example of uncontrolled decline that is intentional and irrational. Sometimes a rational provision of services is accompanied by an irrational means—in this case deficit spending. Irrational budgeting procedures are perpetuated by the very actors who decry the deficit, for it is easier to incrementally continue insolvency than to stop, question the basic premises, and turn the situation around. As with Chrysler Corporation, the turnaround will not occur until the crisis is so near that demise is inevitable unless a sudden drastic change occurs. This incremental insanity is labeled by Argyris (1980) as single loop learning as compared to the rational behavior of double loop learning. Argyris describes incremental planning and budgeting as a single loop learning process since an event occurs, its consequences are noted, changes are made to deal with the consequence, the performance is checked, consequences are noted, and changes are made again to accommodate the consequences. This sequence continues. Argyris points out that this sort of thinking allows for errors to compound at an exponential rate, since the basic error—the premise on which the action was initially set—is never reevaluated. The opposite of single loop learning is double loop learning, which requires a serious readjustment of problem-solving procedures. Double loop learning requires that a decision be made, consequences noted, and if changes are deemed necessary, the decision makers reconsider the premises upon which the original decision was based. This provides a new computation each time a recalculation is made and eliminates correcting one error by making two more.

SUMMARY

• Decline is defined as prolonged suboptimization of an organization's productivity. There are three types of decline, each of which may overlap the other: undiscovered, uncontrolled, and orchestrated. Undiscovered and uncontrolled decline may be either intentional or unintentional. Orchestrated decline is intentional.

• Suboptimization strategies are designed to produce less than best results for a variety of reasons. The reasons may be judged rational or irrational, depending on whose values are maximized by the action.

• Orchestrated decline is intentional from the outset, at least on the part of some subset of decision makers.

• Some organizations experience more than one type of decline. Typically an organization may be in decline that is undiscovered. By the time it is discovered, it may have reached the uncontrollable level.

• No organization is free of the threat of decline. Organizations judged excellent one year may be in the throes of decline shortly thereafter.

• Decline may be used constructively or destructively. It may be used to bring about a metamorphosis that produces a healthier organization in the long run. It may also be used to reallocate resources from one unit to another.

3

The Declination Trend

An organization in decline is far more fragile to manage than one in growth. In growth everyone will potentially gain, but in decline someone is going to lose whether it is a job, position, prestige, status, or profits. Once decline is set into motion, predictable behaviors occur in the work force, behaviors that serve to perpetuate the downturn rather than arrest it. It is for this reason that decline always has the potential of becoming destructive, even if it was originally orchestrated for constructive purposes.

DOWNWARD SPIRAL

Much like the progressive circles of Hell depicted in Dante's *Inferno*, organizational decline can be characterized by stages of severity. Dante depicted nine circles with the first circle being the least horrible and the ninth circle being the most horrible depth to which a mortal could descend. The inferno is a series of concentric circles diminishing in size in a conical fashion until, beneath the ninth circle, there is room for only one—Lucifer (Bainbrigge, 1969). Organizational decline is analogous to the inferno, in which each phase in the downward spiral of the organization is more serious and leads closer to the firm's self-destruction, the organization's Lucifer.

CASE IN POINT: THE NEWSPAPER INDUSTRY

Screenwriter and former Detroit Free Press executive editor Kurt Luedtke explains what happens in the newspaper industry when one appears to be in trouble. He says failing newspapers get caught in a downward spiral such that "once the No. 2 newspaper in a community falls significantly behind the leader in circulation, advertisers desert it in droves, creating an irreversible impression that the paper is headed for the newspaper graveyard" (Randolph & Behr, 1986, p. Aii). As advertising revenues drop off and profits diminish, the newspaper really is in trouble. What may have started as an unfounded rumor becomes true. Circulation drops off and the newspaper is soon at death's door.

The downward spiral marking a declination trend is difficult but not impossible to stop once started. Just as with the circles of Hell in Dante's *Inferno*, each circle deeper in descent is mired more in its own consequences. This promotes a domino effect: One event triggers another, which in turn triggers another, and so downward the decline goes. As the case of newspapers points out, first the perception arises that the organization is suffering. Then financial woes befall it because advertisers and subscribers abandon the "loser" and give their business to a competitor. As a result, the competitor does even better, while the "loser" loses more. As the financial crunch hits, employees feel the pinch. They start looking elsewhere for jobs, since they fear they will lose their jobs where they are. The ones who stay devote an inordinate amount of time to gossiping among themselves about the status of the company, and to wondering what will happen next while the firm continues its downward spiral.

The downward side of the Phoenix Syndrome is characterized by slow, inconsistent decline punctuated on occasion by fitful, shortlived recoveries. The decline gathers momentum as it spirals downward. Predictable behaviors of personnel accompany the decline. Figure 2 provides a model of the behavioral correlates during the downward spiral. From the beginning of the process, they are problem recognition and stress reaction to the acknowledgment. This results in a circling of the wagons, which is an attempt to contain the problem by restricting those who do not know from learning about the situation. This has the effect of restricting the information flow both to the external environment and among employees within the firm. Suspicion mounts and fingers are pointed, with everyone attempting to place blame where they think it may be, preferably away from themselves. Paranoia mounts, employees grow skeptical of others' motives, and morale plummets. Collective rationalizations occur among those in group decision-making tasks. As a result of the restricted information flow and the ill feelings that permeate those aware of the problem, group

Figure 2
The Downward Spiral

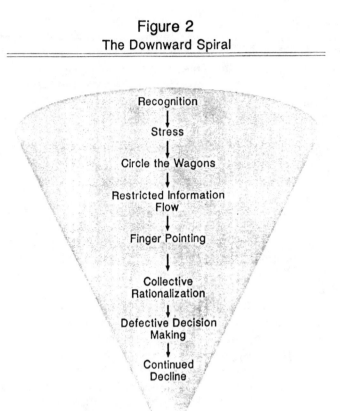

Recognition
↓
Stress
↓
Circle the Wagons
↓
Restricted Information
Flow
↓
Finger Pointing
↓
Collective
Rationalization
↓
Defective Decision
Making
↓
Continued
Decline

reasoning degenerates into a collective rationalization, which avoids addressing the first domino—the actual cause of the problem. It is awfully hard for a firm to pick itself up by its bootstraps when it is unwilling to stoop down low enough to grab ahold of them. The perceived inviolability of the group rationalization produces faulty decisions. Defective decisions are made because the premises upon which alternatives are chosen are faulty. Predictably, this leads to continued decline.

RECOGNITION

In the case of undiscovered decline, the greatest obstacle that executives face is their difficulty in recognizing it for what it is. This is due to a number of factors, not the least of which depends upon the health of the firm. In an up-and-coming optimistic organization, the manager striving for excellence is the manager not only pushing ahead but looking ahead. Starry-eyed visions of success become blinders that prevent the individual from looking to the right, left, and over the shoulder to heed beginning signs of decline. Hints of decline are ignored while energy is focused on achieving the goals ahead.

In an unhealthy organization, insecurity leads to decline through a series of unfortunate events. Organizational insecurity begins the "domino effect" in which a small, seemingly isolated situation gives rise to one event, which then breeds trouble in more parts of the organization. For example, poor communication between management and employees can lead to management retrenchment. The invisible barrier becomes the beginning of more deep-seated problems. Trust gives way to suspicion. This leads to employee unrest, which leads to declining service or product quality. Customer dissatisfaction and declining sales result. For private firms, market share is lost and for public agencies client support diminishes. As morale plummets, valuable employees emigrate to healthier firms while the troubled organization continues to spiral downward (Greenhalgh, 1982; Greenhalgh & Rosenblatt, 1984).

Organizational routines are powerful and tend to obscure signals that contradict standard operating procedures. Messages contrary to those usually received are treated as mild aberrations rather than indicators of trouble. Management-by-walking-around is probably the best way to identify incipient strains of decline. Weekly visits, unannounced and informal, among all levels of employees will yield information different from that which arrives through formal channels—neatly typed in memorandum format. Before productivity numbers noticeably decline, lower level employees can identify issues which, taken singly, may not cause alarm. However, when the same repeated complaint or awareness is mentioned by a number of personnel, it may well be a signal that the dominoes of decline are lined up and ready to fall.

In a commentary on the large number of bankruptcies in the early 1980s, *Industry Week* (1982) cited Abraham Getzler, a consultant for troubled companies. Getzler said that executives of declining companies "have refused to recognize the situation until the house is caving in" (p. 83). Much as rearranging the deck chairs on the Titanic really would not have made any difference in regard to the ship's sinking, perceiving a series of indicators of impending decline as temporary aberrations does nothing to stop the declination trend. For example, such weathering-the-storm strategies as postponing investments, reducing maintenance, halting training, centralizing decision making, raising prices, and leaving positions vacant do little to address the underlying problems (Nystrom & Starbuck, 1984). Likewise, reliance on routines that produce inadequate information can produce devastating outcomes.

CASE IN POINT: NASA'S DECISION-MAKING HIERARCHY

Reliance upon the hierarchical decision ladder at NASA had served the agency well for many previous launches of the shuttle. Depending on the nature of the subject matter, decisions were to be made at Level IV, the lowest level, or be sent up to the appropriate level: Level III, Level II, or Level I. When information was not passed up from one level to another, it was assumed that the level below was in control of the situation and there was no need to inquire further. The routines were in place, the standard operating procedures known to everyone, and the policies straightforward. In retrospect, following the explosion of Challenger seventy-three seconds into its flight, there is strong evidence that indicators had been present for some time that such a system needed adjustment. NASA's compartmentalized deliberation process kept information—such as the presence of cold spots on a booster rocket—from being transmitted to the responsible official, making it easier for them to freeze their commitment to launch. There was a general atmosphere of enthusiasm. No one wanted to be reminded that any kind of accident was possible (Kruglanski, 1986).

A discerning executive can use signs of decline as an opportunity to refine the current course. The recognition of problems on the horizon is more likely to occur when it is to someone's advantage. At the nexus of recognition occurs this paradox: Decline is a mixed value. While it may be good for some, it is not good for others. Resistance to change will come from those who benefit from the existing procedures. Promotion of change will come from those who will benefit by revising existing procedures. Acknowledging who is winning and who is losing is helpful for both formal and informal cost-benefit analyses (Sutton, Bruce, & Harris, 1983). By being aware of who stands to gain and who stands to lose in the decline, it becomes obvious when and where decline had its starting point.

STRESS

At the point when decline is recognized, the dilemma phases into the second stage of the declination trend. This is the point of high stress. High stress occurs at either end of the continuum of recognition—at the end which represents overt recognition or the end which represents subliminal recognition masked with denial. Although a certain degree of stress is necessary to energize people into action, there is a point after which it contributes to faulty decision making.

When attention is constructively focused on the problem, this stage marks a readiness for change. An organization manifests its vitality when it takes advantage of the readiness and addresses the problems in a straightforward, constructive fashion. When the organization is not self-aware, the decline continues.

Elevated stress contributes to the perception of a crisis and undercuts constructive examination of the pros and cons of alternatives. Tjosvold (1984) corroborated this in a study he reports. When he divided experimental subjects into groups, he noted different qualities of decision making. One group faced a challenging problem, one faced a crisis, and one faced a minor issue. Those confronting a minor issue indicated little interest in the task at hand. Those who considered the problem to be a challenging situation were more open to hearing opposing positions of subordinates and were more willing to incorporate opposing arguments into their decision calculus. Subjects in the crisis condition indicated they felt markedly more pressure to reach agreement than those in the challenge situation did. Those involved in the challenging situation asked more questions of the subordinate than did those in the crisis condition, who asked more questions than did those in the minor issue situation. The crisis condition induced in this study produced predictable effects: Those in the crisis experienced higher stress than did the other participants and disregarded alternative solutions suggested by those outside their own group.

Tjosvold's study demonstrates the ability of stress to reduce decision quality. This phenomenon is evident in declining organizations. Recognition of decline evokes organizational responses that create stress. Individuals then respond to the stress in a manner that increases their own stress, which evokes more reaction from the organization and, in turn, induces more stress, and so on in the declination trend (Mohrman & Mohrman, 1983).

CASE IN POINT: STRESS IN DECLINING ORGANIZATIONS

Robert Sutton (1983) reports phenomena he observed in eight cases of organizational decline leading to death. Each of these sites was about to close or had been closed for less than a year. The firms studied were a small independent auto plant, a large auto plant owned by a major corporation, a large department store owned by a chain, a small retail store, a nonprofit hospital, a publicly funded center for the disabled, an academic unit, and a research organization. The stress in the work force contributed to an extraordinary number of rumors, which spread among employees, and of the rumors repeated most often, many were bleaker than actual fact. In addition to the abundance of rumors, another phenomenon was found. The best employees jumped ship as soon as the seriousness of the situation made itself apparent. This happened at all the sites except where the employees were extremely loyal or were assured equal or better positions in the parent organization.

CIRCLE THE WAGONS

As decline is recognized, stress increases. A predictable reaction to this, especially among those at the top of the unit in distress, is a "circling the wagons" phenomenon. The people aware of the dilemma form a huddle. In the huddle they function in a crisis mode, not collecting information from an array of resources, but rather collecting only from those sources who are in agreement with them. Since most top level administrators find something they could or should have done differently to ward off problems, guilt is usually felt by each administrator. This produces feelings of inadequacy and defensive postures. There is a sense of urgency that something should be done. Just as Tjosvold's study showed, decision makers screen incoming messages from those marginal to them and do not freely enter into exchanges with those outside the circle. If managers in the huddle make any changes, they focus on marginal issues rather than reexamining the premises upon which the practices are based. They target the last domino that fell, instead of confronting the instability of the first domino. This behavior occurs whether in a small owner-operated business or in the rarefied atmosphere of the White House.

CASE IN POINT: THE JOHNSON WHITE HOUSE AND ESCALATION OF THE VIETNAM WAR

The decision of the Johnson Administration to escalate the war in Vietnam demonstrates this circling of the wagons. Amidst domestic and international condemnation, President Johnson and his advisors refused to seriously reexamine the premises upon which they justified the escalation. Whenever members of the ingroup began to express doubts about the actions, a predictable pattern emerged. "The dissenter was made to feel at home, providing he lived up to two restrictions: first, that he did not voice his doubts to outsiders ... and second, that he kept his criticisms within the bounds of acceptable deviation, not challenging any of the fundamental assumptions of the group's prior commitments" (Janis, 1972, p. 120). The "club" remained intact by the subtle but certain pressures for conformity and by the exclusion of outsiders.

Management teams perpetuate routines that are dysfunctional because "it's what we're used to, and it worked for us in the past." Humans are not unique in this reluctance to change. Robert Kahn, at the University of Michigan's Institute for Social Research (*Business Quarterly*, 1982) cites an experiment which used rats. Given a choice, rats chose predictable electric shocks over unpredictable shocks even when the predictable shock was three times more intense and nine times longer. In other words, predictable misery was preferred to unpredictable happiness. Predictable problems can fit more easily into a firm's operations than unpredictable risks that may or may not succeed.

Routinization of behavior patterns gives rise to standard operating procedures. Nystrom and Starbuck (1984) use the term "encased learning" to describe this habit. Managers encase their learning in programs and standard operating procedures that can be executed routinely. These in turn generate inertia, which is strengthened when new members are socialized to the routines and reinforced for learning and practicing them. Conformity to prescribed procedures leads to smooth functioning, whether the firm is ascending, maintaining, or declining. Reliance upon proven procedures provides a labor saving cognitive shorthand. Not until staff see overwhelming evidence that these habits are seriously deficient or counterproductive will they consider significant changes.

Organizations in decline are stressful places to work. Employees adopt self-protective behaviors that make it even more difficult to check the decline. The self-protective behaviors threaten the viability of the organization even more so. As a part of the circling of wagons, choices are constrained. The array of alternatives is limited and decline steadily continues. The circling of wagons diminishes conditions for employee involvement and increases employee dissatisfaction and stress.

Management is often unaware of the resources personnel hold for combatting the declination trend. Managers, as all other staff, live in their respective worlds circumscribed by their own cognitive structures (Nystrom & Starbuck, 1984). Without the free flow of information each person's idiosyncratic perceptual system propagates unique explanations and attributions that may or may not be shared by the majority.

RESTRICTED INFORMATION FLOW

The ultimate consequence of circling the wagons is to restrict information flow. Decision makers go into a crisis mode, fall back on the routines they know best, and do not seek or attend to information that is contrary to their own beliefs and opinions. Subordinates who favor a course of action different from the one management selects are seen as interfering rather than as a source of useful information (Tjosvold, 1984). Groupthink takes over. Dissident factions are excluded from suggesting alternatives, offering information, or choosing among alternatives. Decisions are adhered to without question. Decision makers are less interested in hearing arguments from workers when they are in a crisis mode than when they are not. This effectively restricts the information flow from those persons who may know best where critical problems lie.

Management's single-mindedness and unwillingness to use subordinates' opposing ideas promotes the declination trend. In contrast, Contino and Lorusso (1982) report the case of a turnaround in the fleet maintenance and repair shop in New York City's Department of Sanitation in 1979. After a steady decline in productivity, poor quality work, excessive overtime and materials costs, changes were made. Those in management cleared the communication channels between them and all levels of the work force. A climate of mutual cooperation and trust spanning all levels of the organization was created, and an attitude of open-mindedness was encouraged. All levels of personnel contributed information. At the end of six months, productivity was up, and labor and operating expenses were drastically reduced.

It is critical that all segments are included in the flow of information before a declination trend can be stopped. Typically a turnaround occurs more from an infusion of new ideas than from an infusion of funds (Nystrom & Starbuck, 1984). Strategic reorientations are rooted in cognitive shifts. Information from a wide array of sources is necessary to shake loose the perceptions contributing to the declination trend. A sometimes unconscious process goes on among colleagues when things are bleak. Well meaning co-workers and loyal subordinates distort or fail to repeat information that dissents from a respected colleague's point of view.

Because of the tendency to kill the messenger rather than attend to the unwelcome information, people bias their messages to enhance good news and to suppress bad news. To overcome this tendency the receiver of information must encourage dissents and assume they are at least partially valid. This rarely happens. Lorange and Nelson (1987) report the case of a division vice-president who routinely combed his staff for good news to report to management committee meetings. Although serious problems existed in his division, he created and perpetuated a false sense of comfort. An additional consequence of the restricted information flow is to maintain the status quo. By doing this, the decline is ensured—for decline is the status quo.

FINGER POINTING

As the information flow is restricted, suspicions abound. Group identification develops and insulates members from further blame. Finger pointing, which is the process of attributing blame to someone other than oneself, creates a common enemy. Without accurate information to corroborate or disavow gossip, rumors are used to provide answers for the myriad of questions about why things are happening as they are. An atmosphere of mistrust pervades the organization. Staff members try to pin blame on others, not so much for the decline itself but for singular events—such as blaming one domino for falling and ignoring the fact that the others behind it had fallen. As suspicions mount, so does fear. Productivity decreases as employees stop concentrating on their jobs. They concentrate on the flurry of rumors and gain or create answers to allay rising anxieties.

Decline results in a substantial, absolute decrease in an organization's resource base over a prolonged period of time. Retrenchment is a short-lived, purposeful reduction induced to cut expenses and prevent a full-fledged decline from occurring. The difference is a critical one and retrenchment should not be confused with decline. However, retrenchment often generates stages similar to those in the declination trend (Cameron, Kim, & Whetten, 1987). Finger pointing is one of the features they produce in common. For example, Gilmore and Hirschhorn (1983) cite the case of hospitals currently practicing retrenchment and adjusting their management practices to accommodate a prospective payment system.

CASE IN POINT: RETRENCHMENT IN
THE HOSPITAL INDUSTRY

In the past hospitals were reimbursed according to the expenses they incurred. Now hospitals are revamping, for they are being paid a set fee based upon the diagnosis of the patient. This system of retrenchment means that ancillary care givers are being laid off to cut costs. The threat of losing one's job causes suspicion to run rampant. Habits and friendships that were formerly quite congenial are now looked upon with suspicion. People at all ranks are affected by the changes. Those at the bottom feel paralyzed by new uncertainties. While they expect leadership and clarification (i.e. good quality information) from the top, the people at the top become impatient because those beneath them are failing to propose options (i.e. good quality information). A vicious circle of incompatible expectations ensues. When someone at the top finally makes a unilateral decision, lower level staff members feel betrayed because they were not consulted. Then the top feel angry with those below since they (the lower ranks) would not "take the ball and run with it." Thus a formerly workable pattern of decision making evolves into a stalemate with mutual blaming.

A situation suffused with uncertainty is quickly mired in suspicions and finger pointing. Scapegoating occurs, along with attention to insignificant detail, when it is not the detail that matters. Overcontrolling arises, when control is not the issue. Short-term planning is practiced, when it is long-range planning that is needed. And minor aspects of the job are magnified, when these are not the ones that are relevant to the decline.

Awareness of interpersonal relationships is critical to the management of decline. Finger pointing is a sign of the degree of suspicion that exists. People who formerly joked as they passed in the hall circle the wagons around themselves. They avoid discussing serious matters so as not to reveal information that may be beneficial to "the enemy," even though no one is certain who "the enemy" is.

COLLECTIVE RATIONALIZATION

Collective rationalization is a protective belief in the correctness of the group, a belief that what is being done is the best thing to do. Complainers are stereotyped as trouble makers. There are illusions of unanimity and those who voice dissent are excluded from the group.

Although the wagons are circled and the information flow is cut, the lack of facts never interferes with the collective rationalization of the management team. As a group the managers develop a logic that justifies to them why events are happening as they are. Perhaps as much a result of groupthink as anything else, those who should be scrambling to learn all possible solutions are actually busily setting up barriers around a circumscribed set of choices. *Industry Week* presents a discussion of the tendency for managers to surround themselves with those whom they know best: "Surrounded by associates who have worked together for years, company chieftains are all too eager to grasp at straws and accept optimistic rationalizations for current problems . . ."

(1982, pp. 79, 83). This remark is reminiscent of Tjosvold's study. He concluded that those who perceived themselves to be in a crisis are less likely to be interested in hearing arguments from workers compared to those who perceive themselves to be involved in a challenge or a minor issue situation. The crisis undercuts constructive controversy.

Encased learning breeds rigidity that perpetuates itself even when its opposite, flexibility, is required. Standard operating procedures do not apply to all situations and so, even though reliance on SOP's is an efficient mechanism, it is not efficient during decline. Survival, in and of itself, is not easy. According to Nystrom and Starbuck (1984) only 7.5 percent of U.S. corporations survive twenty-five years. Fresh beliefs and values bring a needed turnaround, but in their absence, the same old way of doing things produces the same old result, or worse.

Organizations succumb to the downward spiral of the declination trend when the management team, by recollections of past success, live in worlds circumscribed by their organizational memory and resulting perceptions. A nostalgia for days gone by contributes to a blissfully uncritical evaluation of the organization's past. This love affair with the past prevents management from critically differentiating which historic strengths are real and need to be revitalized from those that are no longer relevant to the current and future environment in which the company finds itself (Gilmore & Hirschhorn, 1983). However, an equally uncritical love affair of change for the sake of newness is also blinding and does not hold promise of stopping the decline over a long-range perspective.

All in all, collective rationalizations are rarely as productive as they are satisfying for those engaging in them. Wanting to believe one way and believing that way does not make it so. It produces a blindness to actual causes and consequences of current procedures. When collective rationalization is used, there are several benchmarks. One is the restricted flow of information into and from those who have circled the wagons. The next is that the social circles diminish in size. Dissenters are expelled from the group and blamed for the ever thickening morass. For example, recall that when John Dean dissented from Nixon's inner circle, his expulsion resulted. Furthermore, those who remained in the inner core then tried to blame him for what had gone wrong.

CASE IN POINT: THE NIXON WHITE HOUSE
AND THE WATERGATE COVER-UP

In an analysis of the taped conversations held in the Oval Office, Irving Janis (1982) reports several findings typical of collective rationalizations: (1) The "Nixon team" of Richard Nixon, John Dean,

John Ehrlichman, and Bob Haldeman had a high degree of concurrence with one another, making them a cohesive group; (2) they
disagreed very little with one another and only rarely debated alternative measures; (3) their discussions were marked by overoptimis-
tic views and they consistently ignored warnings of trouble ahead;
(4) the group shared an illusion of invulnerability whenever
discussing cover-up activities; and (5) they justified their illegal
actions and dismissed the danger of their being exposed.

DEFECTIVE DECISION MAKING

Defective decision making is just as unproductive in stopping decline
as collective rationalization. It is based upon an incomplete search of
alternatives and objectives, and a desperate grab for solutions. Some
managers are schooled in the "organization as strategy" approach to
problem correction. When a problem is seen in only two-dimensional
terms, the vertical and horizontal shape of the firm, much is left out of
an optimal decision calculus. Focusing on structure constrains choices
into a static two-dimensional figure. A firm that is frequently going
through reorganization as a strategy for problem solving is very much
like the child who, once all the dominoes have fallen, sets them upright
so that they will start the process again. In addition to failing to address
the root cause of the decline, such changes usually do more damage
than good when used several times over a several year period. Although
reorganization may result in an initial burst of renewed effort, the
productivity curve falls back into its old pattern when the newness
wears off. Poorly planned reorganizations generate insecurity.
Rearranging the workforce disrupts carefully nurtured personal
relationships and creates friction and finger pointing. This assures the
employees, if they had not known it already, that things are not well.

Good decision making in the face of decline includes at least these
eight steps:

1. recognize which decisions need to be made
2. choose who is going to make them
3. determine goals and objectives
4. identify resources necessary to achieve the goals and objectives
5. define the skills required to achieve the goals and objectives
6. complete a skills list of present staff
7. present several workable options for achieving each
8. make, execute, and implement the decision in ways that are equitable, and
   result in a strong, lean, reorganized, efficient organization (Smith, 1982)

Decision making in declining organizations rarely follows the steps listed above. A paradox of timing occurs: Management is less likely to question cultural norms and learn new responses at the precise time that it should. When in crisis, decision makers are aware of conflicting opinions but are too enmeshed in collective rationalization to incorporate them. They are more likely to emphasize well learned institutional responses. Managers are more likely to look for internal solutions when they should look for external solutions (Cummings, Blumenthal, & Greiner, 1983).

A classic example of defective decision making is that which applies the decision rule: "Last hired, first fired," or "last program in, first program out" (Ketchum, 1982). This LIFO principle fails to acknowledge the advantages of keeping the most recently hired. For example, often these are the personnel who have higher productivity, more enthusiasm, and fresh ideas. Another example are the rules managers use when confronted with the responsibility to cut costs. The two easiest procedures are across-the-board cuts and cutting vulnerable programs. With an across-the-board cut, a fixed percentage reduction is made in the budget of each department. Cutting vulnerable programs involves the newest programs that have not yet built a constituency, or programs that have had public relations problems (Higgins, 1984).

Decline is a multidimensional phenomenon with no one best course of action, either proactive or reactive. Citing the case of colleges confronted with declining enrollments and revenues, Cameron and Zammuto (1983) report that seven of fourteen colleges recovered from decline by finding new market domains. This is a proactive stance helpful in some situations but not helpful in others. Oftentimes organizational inertia mitigates against new activities or new domains being explored.

CONTINUED DECLINE

Circling the wagons, restricting the information flow, and finger pointing are symptomatic of a groupthink mentality producing defective decision making. The group develops an illusion of invulnerability and believes in the inherent rightness of its decisions. This closed-mindedness gives rise to collective rationalization, stereotyping, and denunciation of outsiders who might question its decisions. The members of the group are subtly pressured to conform. Those who dissent receive the message that "if you're not a true believer, you're hardly a believer at all." Dissenters are then excluded from information to which the remainder are privy.

Decisions made by the group reflect an incomplete information search that produces an incomplete survey of alternatives and objectives. Information is selectively deleted from group discussions. Risks of a preferred choice are not appraised thoroughly, and contingency plans, should the preferred decision fail to bring results, are not developed (Janis, 1982). This explains why dysfunctional strategies are continued and decline is perpetuated.

CONFRONTING THE DECLINATION TREND

When the declination trend begins, one of two alternatives will occur: The decline will stop or it will continue until the organization is at death's door. Either of these scenarios can happen quickly or over a period of years. Even when an organization attempts to decline gracefully, it confronts obstacles. Each organization has exit barriers; that is, it has obstacles before it that prevent it from easily and gracefully moving out of the domain and disbanding or vitally changing its mission. Kathryn Harrigan (1982) has written of these exit barriers. They are those factors, either strategic or managerial, that dissuade firms from making smooth, timely exits from their lines of business. The strategic barriers revolve around image issues. It will typically be harmful to a company's image if it chooses to close its product line and exit the market. Managerial barriers are those involving personal/emotional/ prestige investments and turf battles.

Harrigan lists a number of firms that have recognized that at least one of their product lines was declining to the point that exit had to be contemplated. Exit barriers were examined by each of these firms and different strategies were adopted depending upon the unique situations confronting them. GTE Sylvania, Gerber Products, and Dow Chemical adopted a strategy of increasing the investment in the declining product in order to dominate a viable niche of remaining customers. Brown Shoe, Rohm & Haas, and Tennessee Eastman held the product line's investment level rather than increase. With this strategy, the companies could reinvest to maintain their economic posture until uncertainty about the market niche had been resolved. Sunbeam Appliances, Allied Chemical, and Courtaulds, Ltd., pruned particular product lines in order to invest resources to position themselves in the more lucrative niches. General Electric, H. J. Heinz, and S. W. Farber, literally drained the investment of their products to yield the best cash flow without regard for their market position. Raytheon and E. I. duPont de Nemours chose to divest or to abandon assets as quickly as possible.

But not all organizations actually exit the scene. Some bide their time as decline continues downward, only to resurrect the firm almost at its point of demise. Harrigan (1982), after recounting the experiences listed above, admonishes managers that prudent timing and careful analysis of industry traits are critical.

When decline has started, it is healthier to face it and keep the information flow open (Harrigan, 1984). Byzantine management (management which appears to be operating in the light while actually operating in the shadow) is about as successful in managing decline as Byzantine politics were successful in keeping Richard Nixon in office for his second term.

Once started, decline is more likely to continue than to arrest itself. It is imperative that managers understand this and deal with decline as a ubiquitous threat to the health of the organization. Recovering from decline requires that the firm arrest the downward spiral.

The eight stages of decline that accompany the downward spiral of an organization are predictable. At first, financial and/or employee morale loss is obvious. Then finger pointing follows, with the attempt to pin the blame on someone. Usually current management is blamed by outsiders, while current management blames events out of its control. Then the information flow dries up inside the organization and people become hypersensitive to others, to what they are saying, and to whom they are saying it. Next comes a change in management, symptomatic of superficial solutions to deep-seated problems. When firms change management, they become even more rigid. Jeffrey Ford (1980) says that the degree of structure during decline is greater after a new management team takes over than before.

A reorganization of the firm follows, with a tightening of the structure. This is what Ford calls "structural hysteresis." The level of structure, formalization, centralization, differentiation, and administrative intensity, will be greater in the same organization for a given level of size during decline than for the same level of size during growth. Accountability and control are centralized in the hands of a few.

An example of this chain of events occurred at Tampa General Hospital in the early 1980's. As noted in Chapter 1, this hospital chose to cut deficits by turning away patients who had no funds to pay for their care. The course of Tampa General's troubles is almost identical to that of other public general hospitals. "Press reports have suggested the hospital is mismanaged and a new top administrator has been hired," report Fanning and Wiley (1984, p. 26). The scenario went like this:

1. Budget was in the red because third party payment guidelines became more stringent and commercial hospitals turned away indigents so they could keep their own costs down.

2. As soon as the budget was in the red, management was blamed and a new administrator was named (an example of killing the messenger, rather than listening to the message).

3. With the new administrator also came a decrease in services.

4. The patchwork repair was doomed to fail because the basic assumptions about who should provide medical treatment to the poor had changed.

Finally, a commercial hospital became involved, promising it could do things cheaper, and it entered into a contract to manage the hospital.

This is the attempt at (and the promise of) resurrection (Fanning & Wiley, 1984). The recent history of Cooper Green Hospital, the public general hospital serving Birmingham, Alabama, provides another example of the stages of decline.

CASE IN POINT: COOPER GREEN HOSPITAL REVISITED

Cooper Green Hospital is another example of an organization in decline. The hospital serves the medically indigent in and around Birmingham, Alabama. Controlled by the Jefferson County Commission, it has been in a downward spiral for several years. This results largely from the funding problems confronting all hospitals that provide health care for medical indigents, including Tampa General. After publicizing financial figures showing that the hospital was operating at a deficit, the County Commission announced it was dissatisfied with the current operation at the hospital. The first step typical of decline is a change of management. As the first attempt to "take action," the CEO was fired and a new CEO was recruited to clean up the current problems. When the new CEO arrived he faced the usual set of problems. Internally, the hospital was suffering from absentee problems, low employee morale, and high turnover of key people. Recruiting replacement staff was difficult because potential job candidates felt they would be stepping into a beehive to go to work there. The facility was being criticized by the local media. This created a negative image among the public and made paying patients even more reluctant to go there for treatment. The County Commission repeatedly drew attention to the financial problems of the hospital and pointed the finger at the new CEO to clean up the problems.

The climate and culture at the hospital changed. Employees isolated themselves from one another, little meaningful dialogue accompanied discussion in decision-making meetings, and "squealers" were accused of carrying information to the County Commission and elsewhere. Suspicion increased. Predictable behaviors were manifested by staff members, who perceived themselves to be left to twist in the breeze, hanging by a thread. Internally, organization members felt things were out of control with no leverage over resources or staff. The trust level between colleagues became lower and lower as suspicions emerged from an atmosphere filled with anxiety. Meetings formerly filled with camaraderie and exchanges of ideas became quieter and quieter. Employees whispered current rumors to one another behind closed doors so they would not be seen talking to one another. In groups of formerly trusting colleagues, people would not talk because of a nebulous fear that someone might be a plant "of the other side," or of a fear that things might get out of control. Because of the undiscussable nature of almost everything, group decisions were made on less and less factual information and on more and more conjecture, speculation, and unspoken attributions. Factions arose within the hospital with fingers being pointed in all directions. As the decline progressed, it is unclear whether it continued as a function of uncontrollable externalities (poor people cannot pay their medical bills), or as a function of unintentional, uncontrolled decline due to the inability of decision makers to restore confidence and develop a fiscally responsible system.

CONCLUSION

It is more difficult to manage an orderly retreat (read "decline") than it is to manage an orderly charge (read "renewal"). In most cases the reason for the charge is self-evident and the goal is obvious. A retreat, on the other hand, is ambiguous. It is accompanied with the threat of personal harm and it is counter to one's training. There are few rules governing people's behavior during the retreat, and suspicion born of fear is mighty.

The significance of the declination trend is that it does not get started overnight and it will not turnaround overnight. Borrowing from Nystrom and Starbuck's (1984) warnings about organizational crises, similar caveats are applicable to organizational decline:

1. Avoid constricting the information flow. Assume all dissents are partially valid.
2. Keep all information lines open, and evaluate the costs or benefits that would accrue if messages are correct.
3. Try to corroborate all messages to learn which are more likely to involve accurate information.
4. Launch experimental probes that will confirm, refute, or modify the ideas.

The further into the downward spiral that the decline is addressed, the more difficult it is to turn it around. It is up to the management team to combat the instinctive reluctance to face decline. It is helpful if, as in Alan Steiss' (1982) recommendation, policies and programs have natural points in their life cycle where reconsiderations are made. Perhaps salvage specialists should be hired to look for potential decline in agencies and firms and forestall it.

Figure 3 displays a force field of decline. The threat of the declination trend is that forces that would ideally address the decline and stop it, actually perpetuate it because of the stress that results when it is recognized. Paradoxically, the forces that prevent decline from occurring faster are activities that may not be performed with the goal of stopping decline. Usually they are attempting to bring about a change in the organizational milieu for any one of several reasons, only one of which may be a desire to thwart decline.

In conclusion, stages of decline and the behaviors that accompany them are predictable and identifiable. Organizations or segments of organizations may be aware of some of the stages and unaware of others. In some circumstances stages occur almost simultaneously, while in others there is a holding pattern before further devolution.

SUMMARY

• Decline proceeds from a prodromal stage in which the conditions are ripe for the onset of prolonged suboptimization. Unless action is taken to prevent it, the downward spiral begins. At the point when decline is recognized, stress results.

• Reactions to the stress, whether it is self-protective, the fear of not knowing what to do, or the stress of recognizing the need for control, contribute to more stress.

Figure 3
Force Field Depiction

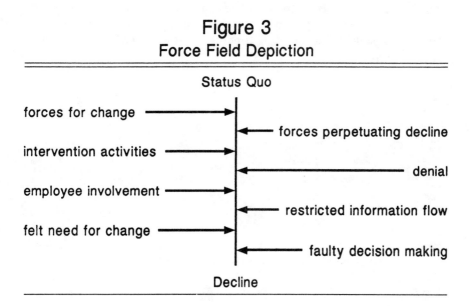

Status Quo

forces for change →

← forces perpetuating decline

intervention activities →

← denial

employee involvement →

← restricted information flow

felt need for change →

← faulty decision making

Decline

• When more than one person is aware of the problem, they circle the wagons, whispering among themselves and disregarding information that is contrary to their beliefs.

• With the diminution of information, come a myriad of rumors and suspicion. The finger pointing and blame which occurs angers those in the outgroup.

• Rationalizations are collectively developed even in the absence of facts. Rationalization contributes to defective decision making since a full array of alternatives are not available and goals may be short of turning around the decline.

• Because of this state of affairs, decline continues.

• Crises, although they test the mettle of the organization, are not responsible for decline. How they are handled, though, may be a harbinger of decline. A resilient, self-confident organization should be able to respond to crises and survive. Crises usually test the organization's ability to maintain, or lose and subsequently regain, public confidence. Such was the case when the ballroom skywalk fell at the Kansas City Hyatt and the American Institute of Architects responded. It was also the case with the Tylenol tamperings when Johnson & Johnson, and its manufacturer of Tylenol capsules, McNeil Consumer Products, moved quickly to respond to the media's clamor for information (Molotsky, 1986; Vickery, 1983). An organization has to provide timely and accurate information to the media in order to keep public perceptions positive and to guard against decline.

• A poorly handled crisis contributes to decline. An organization that has closed itself off from those outside the organization is in trouble. By concentrating on controlling the doubts among its own staff, it renders itself incapable of responding openly to the public's cry for more information.

4

Between Decline and Renewal

The juncture between decline and renewal is critical. It is at this point that decisions and actions result in either the death of the organization or its resurrection. This chapter reviews the elements of decline which lead to the "bottoming out" phase of the decline-followed-by-renewal process. And it addresses effects which decline has on the corporate culture.

When decline is recognized, management is the body with the ultimate responsibility for addressing it. So, when we talk of the Phoenix Syndrome, in which organizations reach all but brain death before their resurrection, we must focus on management. In a description of the decline and ultimate death of the United Fruit Company, Thomas McCann (1976), a former corporate vice president of United Fruit, emphasizes this.

CASE IN POINT: UNITED FRUIT COMPANY

"When a complex organization begins to fall apart, it doesn't all go at once: it isn't like a bomb in the cellar or a plane crash. It happens in bits and pieces, a fissure here, a missing part there. The process starts with the people. They become angry. Or frightened. Or restless. They take longer lunches. They change their work habits; those who worked long hours now work less; those who took it easy begin to show up on time and leave later. They talk a lot about the man at the top" (McCann, p. 181).

Thomas McCann's closing sentence that "they talk a lot about the man at the top" echoes the belief that dealing with the decline is ultimately the responsibility of those at the top.

ATTRIBUTIONS OF RESPONSIBILITY

There are three main explanations for why decline occurs: change, chance, and design. Change occurs at different rates. At some times the environment is turbulent and rapidly changing. At other times, it is relatively calm and change can be forecast far in the future and deliberately planned. The inability to foresee change and deal with it effectively presents a stumbling block to any organization.

Chance is the second explanation for decline. Unforeseeable circumstances will cause market conditions or public demands to change swiftly. Chance, in the form of good or bad luck, is not controllable but significantly shapes the future of the organization. A company in the wrong place at the wrong time has far more hurdles to jump than one that happened to be in the right place at the right time.

Designed, that is intentionally planned, decline is a third explanation for decline. On occasion management willfully orchestrates the decline of an organization, or of a unit within the organization. The objective is either to kill it or let it slump to revitalize it later.

CHANGE

The first of the explanations, change, is exemplified by the way new trends are always on the horizon, simultaneously offering threat and opportunity. The trends that fail to be identified become opportunities missed or unheeded threats. The trends identified and acted upon provide opportunities turned into advantages.

Management's approach to potential opportunities largely determines whether the firm will survive and in what form. In his 1984 President's Meeting address, John H. Bryan, Jr., Chief Executive Officer of then Consolidated Foods, Inc. (and now Sara Lee, Inc.) stressed that most businesses fail, or fail to prosper, because they do not deal effectively with change. He warned that either management does not recognize change coming, or refuses to act even when change makes the need for action obvious. The converse of his warning is that businesses grow and prosper because someone sees change coming and acts to capitalize on it. To demonstrate his warning he cited the case of Continental Illinois Bank, which was rated one of the five best managed companies in America in 1979. Only five years later it was being reorganized by the federal government because it faced bankruptcy. Deregulation had led

Continental Illinois into a new marketplace in which the bank's traditional practices proved disastrous. In contrast, Bryan applauded Citicorp, which faced the same deregulated environment, aggressively pursued the consumer market, and prospered. He warned his executives that in order for a company to prosper, it must manage change and amend its standard operating procedures to fit the times (Bryan, 1984; *Time*, 1985).

An obstacle to dealing constructively with change is that organizations, as well as the people who staff them, tend to cling to yesterday's solutions. Bryan was exhorting the leaders in the corporation to be wary of becoming too comfortable with familiar routines and to be vigilant for changes in circumstances. Paradoxically the more that experience, knowledge, and maturity blend together, the more familiar routines become entrenched and resistance to change occurs. Thus, Bryan's comments focus on the ability of management to sense impending changes and act on them. A similar warning is given by Aaker and Mascarenhas (1984), who speak of the need to have strategic flexibility, with emphasis on the word *flexibility*. Acknowledging the ever present threat of decline, they warn managers to be wary when planning market niches. Defensive strategic flexibility is the wisdom to diversify one's products into multiple markets. If one market collapses, others can still carry the firm.

After several tampering incidents with Tylenol capsules, Johnson & Johnson decided to enclose Tylenol in a tamper proof caplet. This change caused problems for the capsule manufacturer, R. P. Scherer.

CASE IN POINT: R. P. SCHERER CORPORATION

Scherer suffered its first loss in fiscal 1985, and 1986 was bleak as well. It had been producing hard-shell capsules for Tylenol and other drug manufacturers. When Johnson & Johnson decided to discontinue hard-shell capsules in favor of tamperproof tablets and caplets, Scherer could absorb the loss since Tylenol accounted for only a small share of its hard-shell capsule market. After a price war among hard-shell capsule makers, a change in market interest from hard-shell capsules to caplets and tablets, and a decline in enthusiasm for vitamin E capsules as a panacea for skin tone, Scherer was left struggling to stay solvent. It had to decide what niche to occupy. Scherer had a 62 percent share of the worldwide market in soft-shell capsules; however, soft-shell capsules did not take off as Scherer had planned (*Business Week*, 1986b).

The corporation shifted much of its business to manufacturing and marketing encapsulated cough syrup, antacids, and especially fish oil. MaxEPA, concentrated fish oil in capsules, is billed as helping to prevent hardening of the arteries and subsequent heart disease. It gained rapid market acceptance and popularity and is credited with salvaging Scherer's future (Marcial, 1986).

Organizations can be categorized on the basis of their informal norms, such as norms against accepting suggestions, against experimenting, or against taking the initiative. Using these categories as the bases of discussion, one can judge which types are more likely to survive. From an ecological standpoint, firms with norms for being flexible and adaptable are more likely to succeed than those that do not have such norms (McKelvey & Aldrich, 1983). This is akin to categorizing firms according to their strategic predispositions (Miles, 1982). The extent to which an organization exhibits a consistent pattern in the choices it makes about the formulation and implementation of its strategies characterizes its decision-making approach over time. A firm's profile may be drawn by observing (a) the timing and degree of commitment to expansion and diversification; (b) the choices made about acquisition candidates; and (c) the approaches taken to assimilate new businesses and enter new markets. Miles contends that these profiles conform to a conservative versus a risk-taking orientation obvious in a company's traditional domain as well as in new markets.

Economist Lester Thurow faults American industry as a whole for its short-sightedness and its failure to deal effectively with changes that have come about in the transformation from the Industrial Age to the Information Age. He finds three structural weaknesses in American industry that are responsible for predictable, systemwide decline: short time horizons, adversarial labor-management relations, and sloppy quality control. He says:

> When American industries first started to fall behind their foreign competitors, the phenomenon was dismissed as isolated cases of stupidity or bad luck. . . . As the list of industries—shipbuilding, textiles, consumer electronics, steel, autos, machine tools—that have lost out or need government protection to survive has grown, it has become increasingly obvious that something is systematically wrong. (Thurow, 1984, p. 19)

Short time horizons are readily invoked. For example, research and development rarely produces an immediate payoff for a company. Because of this, it is usually the first branch to be eliminated in a period of cutback management. The goal of short-term profit maximization dominates the long-term need to keep up with the rest of the world in new technologies. The result of the short-run success is that it is often followed by a long-run failure. Arguing this point Thurow says:

> Management time horizons are short not because Americans are impatient or stupid, but because we have created an environment where it is individually rational for everyone to have a short time horizon. With high turnover and everyone on his or her own when it comes to economic success, how could anyone expect the American corporation to do otherwise? Corporate time horizons are set by individuals who themselves expect to be with the firm for only a brief time and have, as a result, a short personal time horizon. (p. 20)

Thurow's cure for the continual decline of American industry is that labor, management, and shareholders must think of themselves as partners, each being responsible for maximizing the value of the firm. In this way, each individual has a long-run interest in the survival of the firm, rather than a short-run interest in what the firm can do for him or her.

Adversarial labor-management relations and sloppy quality control hinder American productivity and make American products less competitive in the international market. Managers have been unable to generate an environment in which the labor force takes a direct interest in raising productivity. Thurow says that the key to America's productivity problem lies not among the blue-collar workers, unionized or not, but to its managers and their supporting staffs. The key to productivity lies at the feet of management and it is their responsibility to instill in the work force a desire to work together as a team and produce more and better products.

Management does not need to be told it is responsible. Managers know only too well where responsibility lies. When faced with bad news, they often adopt a defensive posture, deny the problem, and develop sometimes quite convincing scenarios to explain why they were powerless to stop what has happened. Management's collective rationalization is made easier by "circling the wagons," listening only to one another rather than to outsiders, and then building a rationalization that exonerates themselves and avoids looking at the basic cause of the decline. The excuses developed for not having averted decline are similar to these: "it's just a bad season"; "a downtime that will take care of itself"; "the employees haven't been working hard enough"; or "the market will come back when they've seen what the competition produces."

When management persists in destructive habits, it is not just staying in decline, it is causing it. According to Thurow, the decision of the American steel industry to build its last open hearth furnace eight years after the Japanese had stopped using them was unconscionable. Today the American steel industry is behind in technology, cost, and productivity, and has little chance of competing successfully with foreign manufacturers.

Managers risk becoming so absorbed in their own range of vision that their scale of values seems skewed to everyone but themselves. It may seem to those excluded from the "in" group that management has developed fetishes outside the range of the real world. Sometimes they have. But to management it is perfectly rational. Alternative explanations are not examined and information that would yield a different perspective on events is dismissed as having little merit. This is why organizations tend not to change, even when it is obvious to everyone else that critical viewpoints are being ignored (Kaufman, 1971).

Managers react to new ideas as though personally attacked, responding with a variety of reasons why that idea would never work. Transfers and promotions are looked upon with suspicion because no one can be sure whether an ulterior motive is responsible for a proposed move. Pressure builds and people become frantic in an attempt to make everything right. Because of the reluctance to elicit ideas from those outside the circle, fresh alternatives are not developed and the organization becomes even more vulnerable. In Kanter and Stein's (1979) research on the bankruptcy and liquidation of the W. T. Grant Company, they found that the top management of W. T. Grant never tapped the wisdom of its local managers—the ones who could have turned the company around, if anyone could have. Top management failed to include staff in the decision-making process who had information contrary to the standard routines. The company was unable to resurrect itself.

In classic groupthink style, the group of decision makers overestimates the power and rightness of the group. The decision makers collectively try to justify events and dismiss warnings that might force them to reconsider their assumptions. There is pressure on them to conform. Individuals who voice opinions contrary to those of the majority risk ostracism. People censor their own doubts and voice a unanimity of opinion. "Persons who do not fit the dominant organizational stereotype are likely to carry less weight than more traditional types, although the deviants may be free of the mental blinders that limit the conformists' imagination and field of vision" (Kaufman, 1985, p. 50). For example, when the mass immunization to prevent the swine flu epidemic (which never came) was being contemplated in the Ford White House, one expert regrets not voicing doubts about the group consensus to go ahead with the immunization program. "Later, I regretted not having spoken up and said, 'Mr. President, this may not be proper for me to say, but I believe we should not go ahead with immunization until we are sure this is a real threat' " (Neustadt & Fineberg, 1984, p. 228).

Dissent from unanimity is negatively sanctioned, but the consequences of not dissenting are many: (1) an incomplete survey of alternatives; (2) an incomplete survey of objectives; (3) a failure to examine risks of preferred choices; (4) a failure to look again at rejected alternatives; (5) a poor information search; (6) a selective bias in processing information; (7) and a failure to work out contingency plans. The following example demonstrates a state agency in a declination trend with management refusing to address the decline, even when confronted with criticism from observers.

CASE IN POINT: SOUTH CAROLINA DEPARTMENT OF MENTAL HEALTH REVISITED

After several years of public dissatisfaction with the South Carolina Department of Mental Health's operation of its inpatient facilities, the South Carolina State Legislature ordered an audit of the department. On November 16, 1983, the auditors issued a scathing 147-page document reporting that the Department had failed to implement a workable quality control program, and had used short-term planning when long-term planning had been needed. Quoting numerous questionable management operations, it summarized that "Because of the seriousness of these problems, the Council concludes that major changes need to be made in the management of the Department" (p. 2). In its ultimate recommendation, the Legislative Audit Council suggested that "The General Assembly should consider conducting public hearings to determine a corrective action plan to be implemented by the Department of Mental Health" (p. 3).

The Department of Mental Health's retort denied the problems and concluded ". . . [the] Audit Council recommendation for a public hearing is at least premature, if not unnecessary" (p. 147). The management of the Department of Mental Health claimed that the Audit Council had engaged in a witch hunt. The Department then hired a private consulting firm to investigate the department for an "objective" view of the department's operations. On June 29, 1984, The Toomey Company, Inc., of Greenville, South Carolina, issued its report. The investigation looked at the management operations, per se, of the Department, rather than at the result of the management operations, as the Legislative Audit Council had done. The Toomey study team concluded that "There are sincere and serious efforts made to adopt and utilize good management practices within the Department of Mental Health. In fact with a few key changes, the management services will be quite excellent" (p. C-4).

This series of events exemplifies an organization's attempt to kill the messenger who delivers unwanted news. The agency attempted to discredit the quality of the Legislative Audit Council's report by hiring an "objective" firm who would come to more favorable conclusions. The Toomey Company, hired by the agency to critique the agency, found that with a few minor changes (which included centralizing decision making, implementing effective planning, and implementing effective governing board decision making) the agency was in good shape. Furthermore, management's desire to kill the messenger resulted in an even further decline of the agency along with a typical reaction to decline: recognition, stress, circling the wagons, restricting the information flow, fingers pointing at the Legislature for "engaging in a witch hunt," explaining the problems away in a collective rationalization in the form of the Toomey report, and defective decision making continued. In reality, the Legislative Audit Council was conducting the audit because of the Department's continued attempts to disavow complaints from the citizenry and from the staff within the agency. The consequence of hiring a private consultant to say things in a bit sweeter tone and absolve management of blame is an example of the tunnel vision with which management confronted the decline. These events put management and the Agency directly into the center of the declination trend, as if in the eye of the hurricane, where the calmness deludes the participants into thinking that the storm is over.

Concurrence seeking is initiated by those who feel responsible for not having averted the decline. If several people can develop the same collective rationalization, they are more convincing about what happened and how the situation will unfold. This brings management full cycle through the eight phases of the declination trend:

1. recognition of decline
2. reaction of stress to the acknowledgment of the decline
3. circling the wagons in an attempt to contain the problem, or at least contain recognition of the problem
4. restricted information flow, both to the external environment and among employees within the firm
5. mounting suspicion and attributing blame for the problems
6. collective rationalizations are created for explaining why things are the way they are, and what should be done about them
7. defective decision making occurs because the premises upon which alternatives are chosen are faulty

8. phases one through seven lead to continued decline

As management recognizes the problem, or is forced to acknowledge awareness of the problem, it often makes autocratic decisions that seem ill conceived. These faulty decisions reinforce and promote further decline. Stress heightens among all those aware, and behavior in response to the stress promotes further decline rather than putting the firm back on steady footing. Nothing is secure; people are unwilling to stand behind their decisions; uncertainty prevails; and everyone feels threatened. Decisions made by mid-level managers are often countermanded by top management in an attempt to regain control. Morale falls lower, and people feel powerless, as if they are pawns in a system where they have no control.

Management has the choice of denying decline or facing it, and each is threatening in its own way. Specific decisions confront an organization once decline has been acknowledged. One decision is whether or not to do anything. The next decision is what to do. Alternatives address substantive strategic options such as labor cost saving: whether to lay off employees and which ones, whether to introduce an early retirement plan, whether to reduce hours, or whether to cut pay and/or benefits. Debt management also becomes a focus of attention: cost control, deficit financing, and inventory control are means for cutting expenses.

CASE IN POINT: CANADIAN HOSPITALS

Murray and Jick (1985) investigated six Canadian hospitals that were forced to undergo severe budget cutbacks from 1977 to 1982. Although the hospitals were never threatened with closure, they were faced with having to provide services to the same clientele, but with markedly less funds. At the completion of their study the investigators reported that the hospitals had increased the use of outside consultants to advise on how to cut costs. They had also increased the number and length of meetings between department heads and finance experts to explain budgeting realities and justify projected increases. The decision makers relied mostly on tried and true information management systems. There was no new information provided on the effects that the cuts would have on the quality of care provided. As the retrenchments extended over the years, hospital staff increasingly pointed fingers at the Ministry of Health and blamed the Ministry for "political" (in its most pejorative sense) pandering at the expense of efficient health care services.

CHANCE

In addition to change, chance is also responsible for decline. Organizations may fail not because of poor management and not because of change, but because of luck. Kaufman (1985) argues this point succinctly. He summarizes "survival of some organizations for great lengths of time is largely a matter of luck" (p. 67). He says that even the best managed firms fail, sometimes even faster than poorly managed firms. Kaufman cites two reasons for this: the incessant change that accompanies a turbulent environment, and the organization's difficulty in adjusting to the volatility. He argues that chance plays the greatest role in determining which organizations will fail. Therefore, prospects for human control of decline are dim. Furthermore, comparisons between organizations that survive and those that expire because of chance will disclose no significant differences in their respective levels of ability, intelligence, or leadership talents. "Thus, if I am right, the observer who bets on previously demonstrated quality of personnel to assure long organizational life or early death will often be surprised—more often than the observer who bets on sheer luck, good and bad" (p. 71).

CASE IN POINT: BARTLES & JAYMES

In the mid-1980s a new class of bottled alcoholic beverages entered the market: wine coolers. The preponderance of the market, 27 percent, belonged to California Cooler until a sudden switch in public preference occurred. In the first quarter of 1986, Bartles & Jaymes suddenly captured the lead with 27 percent of the market and California Cooler's market share plummeted to 23 percent. California Cooler attributed the rise of Bartles & Jaymes to an aggressive advertising campaign, so they countered with their own aggressive advertising but to little avail (Marinucci, 1986). Fortuitous circumstances ripened the market for wine coolers and Bartles & Jaymes capitalized on it with not only an aggressive advertising campaign but one that captured the imagination of the public. Bartles & Jaymes waited until luck was with them and then they harnessed it. They were in the right place at the right time.

DESIGN

The third explanation for decline is that it occurs by design. In other words, it is planned. Decline of this nature is never labeled as decline. Rather it is called "reallocations of resources," "decrementalism," "cutback management," or some other euphemism. (Which is not to say that all reallocations of resources or all cases of cutback management are examples of intentional decline—just that some are.) Orchestrated decline may be an integral part of either a short-range or long-range plan of the organization. But the orchestration is either couched in other terms, or hidden in the plans so that it is not discoverable and not discussable.

Why would someone want to promote decline? There are at least two constructive reasons: to gain control over a unit, and to energize latent interest groups. In larger organizations that have the luxury of slack resources, decline may be designed and promoted for a particular division in order to be able to divest control of it from those in direct charge. If a unit can be made to fail, or nearly fail, then it is easier to wrest control of it and put it in the hands of the chosen. Just as pouring resources into a unit is a control mechanism with a goal of growth, taking resources away from a unit is a control mechanism with diminution as the goal. Although wresting control of an organization can be achieved, another consequence is that decline will raise the ire of the organization's clientele. This is especially true in public organizations. When constituents organize and protest the withdrawal of funding for an agency, the end result is usually that sufficient funds are reallocated to breathe life back into the agency. Especially in public organizations, cutbacks in popular programs result in vehement lobbying efforts by constituents. People clamor for resources to be reallocated. Congress uses the demand for reinstatement of funding as a barometer to know when to override a presidential veto.

Even when theorists write about decline they couch it in positive terms. An example is George Gilder's *The Spirit of Enterprise,* which is an upbeat discussion of the entrepreneurial spirit. Gilder speaks of losing money in laudatory terms, when it is lost in the entrepreneurial spirit of risk taking in order to turn a potential profit.

A cost-benefit ratio may be developed to weigh the pros and cons of promoting decline in an organization. The constructive side of decline is that it provides needed capital and human resources to focus on a more thriving unit showing greater potential. This is how innovation shapes America's technological future.

CULTURE IN A SQUEEZE

An organization spiraling downward through the declination trend is particularly vulnerable to personnel problems. The culture of the organization is affected by the pressure everyone feels. There are a number of variables that are altered by decline, including management attitudes toward open communications, personal relationships within the organization, and perquisites of employment (Usher, 1986). As any or each of these variables change, the ambience changes and the culture is altered. Culture is most affected by the financial ability of the organization to maintain itself and its style of operation. Changes to accommodate budget cuts such as reductions in staffing or alterations in operating methods have the most serious consequences for organizational cultures. A changed operating environment will alter any organizational culture regardless of attempts to maintain the status quo among personnel.

The impact of budgetary reductions is remarkably similar in the public and private sectors. This is because there are only limited responses available to any organization when it must react to outside economic forces. The immediate response is referred to as "decrementalism" (Levine, 1984). This is the gradual reduction of staff, closing of offices or plants, layoffs (usually involving temporary workers first), reductions in clerical assistance, training, travel, and elimination of perquisites. Decrementalism is effective in cyclical change situations in which the organization must not change fundamentally, but ride out some short-term economic condition. It is not effective when the nature of the economic environment in which the agency must operate is drastically altered. In those situations there must be a basic shift in organizational goals and structure. New products, markets, services, and employee skills are required and the new demands alter the work environment and the culture of the organization to a major degree.

There are special circumstances that affect organizations in transition, regardless of their previous cultural pride. The loss of pride and prestige in the organization is obvious. As the remaining members of the organization view the decline in staffing, power, and influence, they begin to associate themselves with the decline and identify the organization's losses as their own. Then, not wanting to be associated with a "loser," they begin a pattern of behavior identified as disinvestment (Levine, 1984). In this process they separate their own identities from that of the organization and begin to separate personal goals from organizational goals. This is exactly the opposite of the process that establishes a strong organizational culture.

Those organizations with the most nurturing or strongest cultures may be the most adversely affected during decline (Murray & Jick, 1985). This is a function of the employees' having invested in a company that does not live up to their expectations, or a simple loss of faith in the company's abilities and power. Associating with power creates a strong bond in organizational culture. When power diminishes, so does the personal identification that it brings with it. There is no longer a payoff for being part of the company.

Anger among employees is likely to be most intense where there is the least openness about the organization's and its employees' futures (Kanter & Stein, 1979). Euphemisms about streamlining the system, getting rid of the deadwood, and so forth, are not successful for long as masquerades for the actual fact that people are being fired because the firm cannot afford them any longer. Skilled strategic management is called for to minimize cultural upheaval when the organization is threatened with decline. Strategic management involves detecting environmental threats before they extort a price from the culture.

Weaker cultures have less to lose than strong cultures in the process of decline. Members of the group who had little invested in the organization anyway have little to lose. If the prevailing culture is antimanagement to begin with, it will not change much in the process. In fact, a weak culture may even gain some strength as the survivors depend more heavily on each other.

A summary of the problems of culture and budgetary restrictions leads to inevitable conclusions. When an organization faces staffing reductions and changes in objectives and resources it can also expect alterations in culture. Organizations with strong cultures are not insulated from decline. The process of failure can be external to the organization as well as internal. For example, when presidential administrations change, policies change. Public agencies, regardless of their former accomplishments or organizational effectiveness may have resources withdrawn to be reallocated to other efforts. In politically motivated change, the success of a disfavored agency may make it a target for withdrawal of resources. In private sector organizations competition may force a redirection of effort. If the predominant culture is preserved, the organization may be able to regroup behind the new effort. If it is significantly changed, however, a more lengthy process is required for harnessing the culture and directing it toward a new effort.

Even excellent companies fail when they cannot balance goals and culture. Once that failure occurs the organization must modify its methods, strategies, and goals if it is to survive, and must deal with the effects of change on the organization's culture. The overriding consequence of budget restrictions, downsizing, retrenchment, and other organizational changes is alteration of the organization's culture. The general goals of the agency or company may be the same, much of the staffing the same, and the workplace relatively unchanged, but attitudes and investment will not remain constant. Each of the managers and employees will remember and measure the organization's future dealings in terms of the failures of the past. A new culture will be built from the older one and modified as newer members are absorbed and new experiences are added. Although cultural change can be viewed as a continuum evolving with time, abrupt negative changes interrupt the evolution, producing a stressful discontinuity.

When people feel panicked and unsure, employees spend more time speculating with one another than on active productivity. The decline of Farm Products Corporation serves as an example of this.

CASE IN POINT: FARM PRODUCTS CORPORATION

Stein (1979) describes the story of the decline of Farm Products Corporation. Although not machinated, management had to cut expenses in the firm.

> Rumors were rife, jokes were bitter or sardonic, and the most visible sign of activity was the endless scheduling and rescheduling of people as they rushed from one meeting to another, meetings at which, because too little information was available, plans were being made that were unlikely to be carried out because of subsequent decisions that would render them obsolete or inappropriate. Nor was there any great prospect of getting the kind of information that would enable serious planning. (p. 399)

Decline is perpetuated by comfortable but dysfunctional routines and cultural norms. As people work in the same firm over the years, they develop routines that at best promote efficiency and predictability, but at worst, promote cumbersome, outdated, inefficient ways of doing things. Those accustomed to the old way of doing things have a trained incapacity to reexamine their practices and adapt them to contemporary needs. These old hands may be a central source of the problem within the organization and may block attempts to change things, even if that change is designed to prevent entering a declination trend. These norms and habits produce a stress on the system. The stress becomes an insidious phenomenon, in and of itself.

> [Organizational stress] is the process by which a firm or institution . . . becomes deformed, slowly and systematically, by the constant malfunctioning of some system. For a while, other systems take up the load and new, unofficial ways of adapting develop. Possibly the firm as a whole may benefit from the changes, especially if they are recognized as the results of inexorable and inevitable pressure, and the new ways are adapted into the firm's procedures. . . . But often, the firm fights against the deformities. (Weir, 1975, p. 167)

The firm usually responds by rallying the forces to the memory of the good old days, and loyalists reaffirm that the old medicine used to work fine and will again if given enough time. This is possible, but in order to truly pull out of the decline a substantive change must occur. If the original enthusiasm can be conjured up once again, there is a good chance the prognosis will be good. Condor Computer Corporation is an example of a firm that lost its footing after becoming successful. It expanded in areas that were not consistent with the culture of the firm. As of 1986 it had retrenched and come back as a reincarnation of its original self.

CASE IN POINT: CONDOR COMPUTER CORPORATION

From 1977 through 1984 Condor Computer Corporation flourished. In the summer of 1985, it encountered financial difficulty after a series of questionable business decisions started a decline that almost produced its death. Like many of the rapid growth companies dealing in computers and software, Condor had been growing fast, adding staff, and looking for ways to expand. Condor's new president Gerald T. Moore said, "Condor got itself out of control. The company expanded its staff too quickly, didn't control pricing and made deals that didn't relate to the cost of the product" (*Government Computer News,* 1986, p. 57). After substantial losses in 1983 and 1984, the company was able to revive itself, show a profit in 1985, and continue its resurrection into 1986. Moore credits a specific decision with this turnabout. In early 1985 Condor decided to go back to what it could do best: data based management software. Moore says Condor has cut its spending rate, developed a rational pricing and discounting policy and reinstituted a product development program that had been halted in 1984 when the financial crunch came. Condor has established a user newsletter to maintain contact with its users and it has developed contractual arrangements with the U.S. Air Force, the Internal Revenue Service, and Zenith Data Systems Corp., as well as the National Weather Service. Condor has strengthened its technical support, and has adopted an aggressive marketing approach.

BOTTOMING OUT

The story of the decline-followed-by-renewal process is actually a story of how too much of a bad thing can be good. Too much of a reduction in market share or public support stops management from being able to ignore decline any longer. Sometimes things have to go from bad to worse before attention will be focused on how to constructively deal with the problem. End game runs are strategies for dealing with an organization so deeply mired in decline that drastic action must be taken (Harrigan, 1980).

Discussing an organizational deathwatch, Kanter and Stein (1979) ask the question, "Ought an organization have the right to die—to shut down units that may have value to the people in them and that may operate quite effectively, solely on financial grounds?'' (p. 384). This question springs from the sense that an organization has an obligation to the community in which it operates, as well as to its shareholders. For example, when firms are intent on divesting themselves of certain branches, they sometimes try to find absolution for their intention by creating decline as a straw dog. When a firm wants to divest a branch, but knows it will be criticized by the public for closing, it will manage that branch in such a fashion that more money is lost than would ordinarily be the case. This bolsters the assertion that the unit has to be closed because it is threatening the solvency of the rest of the organization. For those who see through the charade there is anger. Discussing the recently announced closing of a particular plant of a large industrial firm, Alfred Slote (1979) quotes the thinking of one of the firm's top executives: ''You bastard, you could have started ten years ago by putting some money in as well as taking it out. You let it get cancer and now you're curing it by killing it'' (p. 414).

Possible end game strategies are (1) increasing the investment in order to seek dominance in the market niche; (2) holding the investment level so that repositioning can be possible with short notice; (3) shrinking selectively; (4) milking the investment for all that it can produce before terminating it; or (5) divesting now. These strategies are designed to be used when an organization sees that it, or a portion of it, is losing its market due to changing technology or consumer demands. End game runs are designed to be used to make the best of a bad situation. Eastman Kodak Company and USX decided in 1986 to shrink selectively and refocus in order to stem decline.

CASE IN POINT: EASTMAN KODAK COMPANY

This century old company operated without showing a net quarterly loss in more than fifty years until the final quarter of 1985. It reported another quarterly loss of $12 million for the second quarter of 1986. Kodak took $167.8 million in unusual costs in the period from 1985 to 1986 as it reassessed its operations. Kodak spokesmen were quoted as saying "the faster we make the changes the better it will be for all parties" (Associated Press, 1986b, p. C3). The tremendous changes the company underwent represented a strategic reassessment of where the company's strengths were and how to recapture them. Kodak paid a $494 million charge for its court-ordered withdrawal from the instant photography business. It trimmed its workforce by 10 percent and absorbed a cost of $43.1 million for its workforce reduction program. It closed a plant in France, bought back some bonds before their maturity dates, and made write-downs and write-offs. A year later, earnings had increased impressively. In 1987 the company reported second quarter earnings of $362 million—a far cry from the second quarter losses of $12 million reported in 1986 (Lappen, 1987).

CASE IN POINT: USX

Finding itself in a dilemma similar to that of Kodak, USX, formerly United States Steel, cut salaries and benefits by 10 percent for managers and nonunion personnel. The chair of the company, David Roderick said "I believe the action we are now taking may one day be regarded as the most painful, but most corrective, of all the steps made in our mission to restore the corporation's prosperity" (United Press International, 1986b, p. B3). Roderick has laid off thousands of workers and converted an historic steel company into an integrated petroleum producer. By 1989 he boasts that the company should have an excess cash flow of $1 billion each year, after capital investments (Merwin, 1987). If this happens, Roderick will truly have turned the company around.

The particular strategy chosen depends on the circumstances surrounding the operations of the firm. End game runs are essentially acknowledgments that everything in the marketplace changes over time and good management includes the knowledge of how to make a successful end game run. Some of these strategies require orchestrating decline within a particular unit in order to keep other branches running smoothly. Critical to the success of the end game is the selection of the right manager to do the job, how to motivate the managers to carry through the end game, and how to evaluate the performance of the declining business in order to know when to exit (Harrigan, 1984).

Filing for bankruptcy to allow for reorganization is the ultimate end game run. It allows a financially failing firm to continue in operation and maintain whatever goodwill it possesses in the community, rather than liquidate its assets. The purpose of the reorganization process is to set aside the firm's liabilities so that debts can be restructured and operations can be continued. At its best, this gives the company a chance to reevaluate its manner of doing business and get a fresh start, having learned from its mistakes (Altman, 1983; Platt, 1985).

SUMMARY

- Ultimately managers are people with pride, jealousy, competitiveness, skills, and weaknesses. They fall prone to trained incapacities in their work and are more likely to be interested in short-term gains compared to long-term gains.

- Goals, power, and prestige are prime motivators for managerial activity. When all else is failing, saving face becomes a driving motivator. For example, the efforts of the South Carolina Department of Mental Health to redeem itself after a scathing critique by the Legislative Audit Council resulted in its hiring consultants to come into the organization and reevaluate the summary and recommendations of that report. Top management denied problems and simply went looking for someone to come in and say that their management was good.

- Regardless of the original cause of the decline, all organizations are collectivities with identifiable boundaries, internal norms, authority ranks, and communications systems. They are goal-oriented, at least to some degree and to some set of goals. So when decline becomes identifiable to those within the firm, certain conditions arise as outlined in the phases of decline. The declination trend can be arrested in any of these phases, but it is difficult.

- Change, chance, and design account for why decline occurs in organizations. Changes in the environment force an organization to stay abreast of trends and respond to them successfully. Sheer luck accounts for the failure of some companies. Being in the right place at the right time produces as many successful companies as being in the wrong place at the wrong time has killed. Orchestrated decline is intentional decline brought about purposefully.

- The culture of an organization changes when it has bottomed out. Interpersonal relationships suffer as well as relationships between staff and the company itself.

- An organization that has bottomed out has gone to the depths of the declination trend. The next stage is to dissolve or resurrect itself.

PART II

THE UPSIDE OF THE PHOENIX SYNDROME

5

Preparing for Renewal

CYCLICAL EVOLUTION

An organization's life evolves in cycles during which various forces differentially exert themselves. Each cycle has a unique set of characteristics. Political, technological, economic, and cultural forces exert pressure in waves, forcing the organization to constantly adapt to crosscurrents and variations. Political cycles center on questions of centralization versus decentralization, popularity of the organization's mission, regulatory environment, tax codes, and power structures. Technical cycles focus on changes in state-of-the-art manufacturing, service delivery methods, or productivity improvement techniques. Cultural cycles represent changes in consumer demands, values of the workforce, acceptable supervisory styles, and environmental concerns. Economic cycles vary according to the strength of the dollar, interest rates, and consumer buying practices. Competitive cycles vary according to the density within the market niche (Kimberly, Miles, & Assoc., 1980).

Political forces constitute one set of conditions. Schmidt and Abramson (1983) put these in an interesting framework in terms of public agencies. They categorize agencies into one of four types, depending on the degree of public consensus about the agency's mission, and the public's perception of the agency's credibility based upon program performance. The types represent combinations from high consensus–high credibility, to low consensus–low credibility. They argue that those agencies perceived to be in decline are those that have two characteristics: There is low consensus that the government should be involved in the task, and the services provided have low credibility because the level of program performance is perceived to be poor. Political failure is the inability to achieve and maintain legitimacy of a strategic constituency. Those that are thought to be successful are those about which there is a high degree of consensus that their missions are within the proper scope of governmental activity, and they are performing at a high level.

Based on these criteria the U.S. Departments of Treasury and State are successful organizations. The U.S. Office of Economic Opportunity is an example of an agency that never met with high consensus and never had much credibility for its program performance level, and it is an example of an organization that went into decline, never to resurrect itself. On the other hand, the U.S. Environmental Protection Agency is an example of an organization with a high consensus that its work is the rightful province of government. However, it is an agency that wavers between being ineffectual and effectual in its program performance because its priorities change with the political winds. Political changes herald environmental changes. Changing executive administrations, whether at the local, state, or national level, cause profound changes in the regulations that constrain or enlarge the scope of organizational activities.

Technological cycles are sometimes predictable and sometimes unpredictable. Technological failure results in the inability to maintain efficiency and competitiveness. An organization that fails, for whatever reason, to stay close to state-of-the-art technology loses out to its competition. But just introducing technology to an organization is no assurance that it can revive itself. Technological change must go hand in hand with administrative change to accommodate the adjustments that take place with its introduction. Otherwise one problem is only replaced by another.

Economic changes are external forces that affect the organization. When the value of the dollar decreases and interest rates go up, more of the company's resources must be expended to pay off debt, thus taking funds away from real growth. For example, the inflation of the late 1970s changed the rosy picture of many organizations. Another change in the economy came with the transition from a manufacturing economy to a service economy. In the 1980s this has produced turmoil in many companies. With greater reliance on service industries and imports, American organizations that in prior times were bulwarks of stability have found themselves frightfully close to death.

Competition is an economic force that emanates from the external environment and changes the picture of the marketplace for any firm. Fierce competition keeps an organization alert, while lack of competition often breeds complacency, which works to the detriment of the organization. With the divestiture of AT&T, long distance telephone service rapidly became more competitive, with AT&T forced by the market to become more responsive to customer complaints and requests for service. New companies sprang forth, offering competition to a company that had never before been accustomed to competing.

Market changes also occur in the environment and have a distinct impact on the niche that the organization controls. When competition comes on the scene, an organization must "work smarter" and "market smarter." When consumer demands change, an organization must quickly reassess what it has to offer the consumer and decide what modifications, if any, are necessary. The American automobile industry and the American steel industry are reeling from the quantity of imported automobiles and imported steel.

Hirschman (1970) discusses consumers' reactions and actions in response to their displeasure with a product. In *Exit, Voice, and Loyalty*, he says consumers affected by an organization have three alternatives. The first is to exit when dissatisfied. If they do not like a product, they simply refuse to purchase it. They exit the market. The second alternative is to give voice. In other words, when dissatisfied, the consumer has the option of verbally expressing displeasure, which warns the organization so that it can do something about the dissatisfaction. An example of this was the public outcry in 1985 when Coca-Cola attempted to introduce what they dubbed "New Coke," which was the generations-old soft drink, Coca-Cola, but with a modified formula. Loyal fans of Coke gave a deafening outcry, forcing Coca-Cola to offer the original formula once again. The third alternative of consumers is loyalty. This is the alternative usually chosen when one cannot exit. It is practiced in conjunction with voice. In the United States the political party out of power typically chooses this option. Rather than leave the playing field, the party plays the role of the loyal opposition, voicing dissatisfaction with administration policies, but remaining loyal to the system. Ideally, an organization will stay flexible enough to be responsive to voice, in order to retain the loyalty of the consumer.

Cultural forces produce changes in what the workforce and the market expect. Cultural failure is the inability of the organization to foster a coherent set of attitudes and values that promote its success. The values of a group evolve and an organization that has not kept pace with this evolution finds itself losing its productive members. Women entering and remaining in the workforce are changing a number of assumptions about the configuration of consumer demands and the value of women as employees. Employment of wives and mothers has increased the demand for quick-to-prepare dinners, childcare centers, and house cleaning services. Comparable worth issues are making a mark on previous low-paying jobs filled primarily by women.

Whether a force is political, technological, cultural, economic, or competitive, an organization is like Pauline tied to the railroad tracks. Decline is always a threat and it is up to vigilant management to see the on-rushing train and remove Pauline from the tracks before it is too late.

PROACTIVE MANAGEMENT

Resurrecting an organization from almost certain demise is a process characterized by several well executed movements: responsiveness to plural environments, development and maintenance of metanorms that sustain the work force through the renewal process, harnessing the efforts of movers and shakers in the organization, and exerting the right leadership at the right time. All of these steps constitute proactive management.

The Phoenix Syndrome only occurs in those declining organizations that resurrect themselves. Some organizations never pull up out of decline. This discussion is about those that do. Although it risks oversimplification, the continuum of proactive to reactive management actions helps explain the difference between those declining organizations that linger and finally die versus those which renew themselves.

Organizations that only react, never able to control the situation in a proactive sense, are more likely to continue spiraling downward until their death. Those that keep abreast of events and take a proactive approach to changes in their external and internal environments are much better equipped to resurrect themselves. This proactive norm indicates that leaders of the firm are looking ahead while also looking to the sides, keeping check not only of what is happening, but also on that which is about to occur. This vision actually serves as a metanorm. It reinforces alertness to changing conditions and a proclivity to make things happen, rather than a proclivity to just have things happen and then react to them. Herbert Kaufman (1971) calls this sort of metanorm a magnetism binding members together. This is also what Ouchi (1981) is talking about in his formulation of the Theory Z organization. The metanorm serves as an overarching norm. It is a driving force that, though indefinable and intangible, is a compelling force within the organization. An organization with a proactive stance toward its milieu may go through revolutionary changes and still survive. The metanorm holds the organization together while it moves from one steady state to another and reestablishes itself.

CASE IN POINT: FEDERAL EXPRESS REVISITED

The story of Federal Express is a story of growth, decline, almost demise, and subsequent resurrection (Tasini with Bernstein, 1987).

In his book about Federal Express, Inc., called *Absolutely, Positively Overnight,* Sigafoos (1983) explained how management saw decline and corrected it before it trapped the company. Reorganizing the structure, bringing different kinds of leaders into the company, and changing from decentralization to centralization, all contributed to the resurrection of Federal Express. Its CEO, Fred Smith, had to make difficult choices about what sort of managerial stance the company should take in its ordeal to avoid bankruptcy. Smith's strategies of changing the organization as it grew to ward off decline now provides lessons in how a company has to stay away from death's door. Although certain aspects of the culture have to be retained in order to keep momentum, managerial and structural changes must take place. A metanorm that reinforces the courage to make difficult choices, maintaining what is good while getting rid of that which is no longer functional, is essential.

Resurrection begins with recognition of the decline and a determination to stop the downward spiral and turn it around. A critical step in resurrection is making all the movers and shakers in the organization aware of the problem and intent upon working in the same direction to stop the decline and revitalize the organization. Harnessing the efforts of the trend setters is critical to the resurrection. Although there are many different strategies for getting critical staff committed to the renewal effort, the first step is to make everyone aware of the problem. Cameron, Kim, and Whetten (1987) state this clearly: "With rare exceptions, organizations are turned around only after the internal organizational and personal consequences of decline are so pervasive and severe that a consensus around the need for drastic action grudgingly emerges" (p. 225).

One tactic that typically gets the attention of employees is to cut the operating costs of the firm. This usually affects each employee in one way or another and makes each personally aware of the decline. Cutting operating costs may range from cutting inventories, to cutting salaries and benefits, to layoffs, to other belt tightening maneuvers. In 1982, *U.S. News & World Report* reported that Massey-Ferguson, an international farm equipment maker, had adapted to hard times by reducing its work force from 67,000 at the end of 1977 to 34,000 five years later. Cutting costs brought about recognition of the problem. People rally when they perceive a crisis, but rarely before. Although Massey-Ferguson teetered on the financial edge for several years, it emerged in 1986 with a new name, Varity, and a renewed dedication (Gilbert, 1986).

On the national political scene, the U.S. Congress has essentially cut operating costs. By cutting domestic spending, programs that touch the lives of most American families have been affected. This has produced awareness that the nation's economy is in decline. Additionally, the Gramm-Rudman-Hollings Bill (P.L. 99-177) wields an impending threat to trigger automatic across-the-board cuts. This threat serves as a reminder to Congressional budget makers to keep the budget under a given target or invoke indiscriminant cuts that no one wants, especially their constituents.

Americans respond to pleas of decline when they choose a President every four years. They elect the candidate who is most persuasive at convincing the voters that the nation is in decline BUT who is simultaneously convincing that he is the one best person to revitalize it. The candidate who loses is either not persuasive enough that the nation is in decline, or not persuasive enough in his argument that he is the one who can turn it around. In 1976 Jimmy Carter promised a distrusting electorate that he would restore vigor and honesty to national government. He won the election. In the 1980 campaign, Ronald Reagan promised an overheated, inflated economy that he would return America to "the good old days" and renew the vigor of the nation. He won the election. In the 1984 campaign, Walter Mondale tried to convince the voters that the nation was on a one-way spiral downward in terms of the national debt, but was not convincing enough to persuade voters that he could or would do something about it. He did not win the election.

Timing is critical during resurrection. Heroes emerge when the electorate or any affected body of people perceive themselves to be in danger. Ronald Reagan was perceived to be the hero of the United States economy during his first term in office. Lee Iacocca is the hero of Chrysler Corporation. In fact it seems that timing is more critical than substance in creating a hero. Those who are convincingly persuasive that they have the answer to people's problems become heroes. This usually follows a prior leader's attempts to resurrect the organization but before the people affected perceived themselves to be in danger. It is not until people are ready for a change that a change can occur and be successful.

The notion of resurrection is the notion of evolution downward met by a revolution upward. At the point of bottoming out, it is relatively easy to be a hero by appearing on the scene once everyone has decided revolution needs to occur. For example, Franklin D. Roosevelt came on the scene when people had reached a consensus that the economy was suffering, too many people were out of work, and things had to change. Ronald Reagan came on the scene when people had reached a consensus that things had to change. The electorate hungered for a sense of decisive world leadership and a halt to inflation. Lee Iacocca took over the reins of Chrysler when company chieftains and stockholders alike had become aware that a drastic change had to occur.

Following a severe performance decline, individual leaders can make a noticeable impact if, under their guidance, the organization revives itself. Leaders are simply not as noticeable when things are going well as when they are responsible for moving the organization upward. Patients may not remember a physician who treated them for a cold or the flu, but they will remember the physician who treated them for a life threatening disease.

There is no one best way to resurrect an organization, an electorate, or an economy. Resurrection style is at least somewhat determined by the simultaneous mix of environments: political, technological, cultural, economic, and competitive. Just as there are externally and internally generated forces that make an organization decline, there are also externally and internally generated forces that push for renewal. Sometimes waiting for these renewal forces to come together is more efficient than forcing renewal before the time is right. The case of Russelsteel, Inc. proves this point.

CASE IN POINT: RUSSELSTEEL, INCORPORATED

Hurst (1984) describes a management team that was suddenly confronted with decline. He explains how the managers had to change their approach, or at least add to it in order for the company to stay alive. Being accustomed to what Hurst calls managing by "hard boxes," that is, by thinking in terms of numbers and analytic decision making, the management team at Russelsteel found itself confronted by a chaotic environment. Units were declining in spite of their well planned strategies. The team decided to try incorporating soft processes, "bubbles," into its decision process. "Bubbles" refers to those "soft" people processes: getting a team to gel and work together, developing trust, being frank with one another rather than saying what everyone thought the other wanted to hear, and practicing management by walking around (MBWA). The team learned how to prepare in the box and wait in the bubble in terms of timing. Managers would plan strategically as they had learned in their training and experience but would consider the people factors involved, such as timing of changes and so forth. Waiting until the time was right meant not implementing until people were ready for it. In the long run they found this saved time because there was no resistance.

A consequence of this network information process is that we often have to wait for the right time to make a decision. We call the wait a "creative stall." In the old organization it would have been called procrastination, but what we're doing is waiting for some important players to come "on-side" before making an announcement. (Hurst, p. 82)

In support of Ouchi's (1981) belief that trust is central to a smoothly running organization, Hurst says trust reproduces itself: "When trust is present in a situation chain reactions occur as people share frameworks and exchange unshielded views..." (1984, p. 85). The more tightly knit the group is, the more likely it is that the sharing of views will generate a shared vision and common purpose.

FORCES FOR RENEWAL

Forces exist for renewal, both inside and outside the organization (See Table 2). The challenge is to identify and use them. Clear goals, leadership, open communication, a "can-do" culture, technology, and adaptability all provide positive forces for renewal. When these are not harnessed in time, filing for reorganization or merging offer alternatives that still provide incentives for the organization to renew itself.

Clear Goals. The purpose for organizing is to accomplish a particular goal that no one person can accomplish alone. It is not unusual for a firm to lose sight of its goal as day to day events consume the workforce's time and energy. Because the goal serves as a unifying force, it contributes toward revitalization when everyone is aware and focused on it. It provides a constructive target.

An organization in decline needs to do two things in regard to its goal. It needs to make certain that the goal is in clear focus to everyone in the workforce, and it needs to make certain that the goal is still timely. An

Table 2
Forces for Renewal

1. Clear goals
2. Leadership
3. Open channels of communication
4. Can-do cultural norms
5. Up-to-date technology
6. Adaptability
7. Reorganization or merger

initial inspection of decline confronting an organization should determine whether the organization is serving a need. Occasionally organizations find themselves in decline because they no longer serve a useful purpose. Whether a firm is succeeding or failing at achieving its stated goal, it has to serve someone's need to be viable. For example, Rooney (1980) cites the case of skid-row rescue missions. After studying them from the vantage of a participant observer, he concludes that they stay in business by continuously failing to achieve their stated mission of converting street dwelling alcoholics to "God-fearing" Christians. Rooney says the missions fail miserably in this task since the derelicts come to the missions for food and a warm bed, and simply go through the motions of worship in order to get what they want. He argues that this is an example of organizational success through program failure. The missions fail to exert any significant effect on the conditions they address. He says this is not unique to skid-row organizations. "Prisons, welfare departments, and mental hospitals may expand inasmuch as the program is ineffective, necessitating retention of those in treatment. . . . [T]he enforcers of drug and gambling laws as well as rescue missions continue because they fail to reach members of their client group" (p. 918). The point is that the ostensible mission of the organization is not the goal that is actually pursued. The mission, however, serves as a rallying cry to support the activities of the organization. The relevance of this for the Phoenix Syndrome is that some organizations may appear to be bottomed out and at the point of death when in fact that is their usual way of functioning.

A deeper look at this succeeding by failing is explained by Mauss (1982), who contends that skid-row missions are actually succeeding because they are meeting the needs of community philanthropists. These benefactors feel a need for the missions and are willing to support them. The missions fulfill needs of clerical dropouts who are only marginally acceptable to mainstream clergy but perfectly acceptable in the world of the skid-row derelict. And the missions fit the needs of the derelicts for food and shelter. Mauss contends that the formal goals of the mission are perhaps misstated, and the informal goal to satisfy a convergence of needs on the part of the community, derelicts, and clerics, is being met. Thus the mission is meeting a need. All this is to say that an examination of the functional needs that the organization satisfies may not be as they would appear. In other words, while an organization may appear to be in decline, the decline may be subjective rather than real. Or, although an organization is meeting its ostensible goal, it may be in decline since achieving that formally stated goal is not actually meeting the needs of the organization's benefactors.

Leadership. Leadership is critical to resurrecting an organization. Factions will exist in any firm, and some will benefit from a change in the status quo, while others will suffer. It is the task of leadership to persuasively convince factions that it is in their best interest to actively participate in the resurrection of the firm.

Sir Reay Geddes talks about the increased challenges that beset chief executive officers in contemporary organizations (Stieglitz, 1985). He says that managing is becoming a more uncertain art because of the emphasis on worldwide communications and the critical nature of time. Management can no longer afford the luxury of taking time to solve problems. While a CEO used to be able to identify a problem and allow a subordinate to do something about it, the CEO must now practice "hands on" management. The CEO has to practice closer surveillance and stay on top of everything that is happening. In terms of the modern work force, Geddes says that management used to assume loyalty, but that is a luxury of the past. Now management must create loyalty and nurture it.

Sometimes organizational learning is the process of correcting a mismatch and making outcomes and expectations match. Ramirez (1983) works on the premise that complete understanding does not precede action, rather understanding develops over time. This paradigm for learning is rooted in action and avoids relying on stereotypes and misconceptions. The traditional way of doing things is for management planning and research to specify what should be learned. Active learning, on the other hand, specifies what planning and research management should be doing.

There is a critical difference between making a decision and taking a decision in the resurrection process. Making a decision occurs in meetings, consultations, and analyses. Taking the decision is wholly a management responsibility and is an active endeavor requiring communication, participation, and monitoring to see if expected results follow.

In addition to emphasizing the skills of the CEO, good management requires reevaluating the formal structure of the organization. Matrix type structures have been lauded as a way of including the maximum number of employees in the decision-making process, but they require time-consuming meetings and produce a burdensome communication process. Control is truncated and lines of authority and responsibility are confusing. Horovitz (1984) suggests that it is time to sound the death knell for such inefficient structures. He calls for replacing matrix structures with cleaner, simpler structures that are strategically more manageable and have improved information systems and a better balance between line and top management.

Although it has faults, a lean hierarchical structure continues to be the most preferred mechanism for controlling a large group of persons engaged in pursuing a common set of goals. By comparing the 1960 and 1970 values of 62 nations regarding aspects of change and stability in four dimensions of bureaucracy, Clarke (1983) concludes that there are few significant shifts in the utility of bureaucratization. Citing a correlation coefficient of .93 between values a decade apart, Clarke says that bureaucratization is here to stay. Even among the developing nations, control is control and bureaucratization is the best method and structure yet developed for maintaining it.

Top management's role is to set policy and guide the firm. Dalton, Lawrence, and Greiner (1970) list what they see as six critical steps in turning around an organization, and each of these relies upon the centrality of management. The first step is the desire by top management to take action. The second is to consider new alternatives to the problem, which often requires new ideas to be generated by someone who is not enmeshed in the reasoning that contributed to the decline. The third step is to identify conditions that led to the problem. Information gathered from all levels of the organization produce this insight. Fourth is to develop solutions and generate a commitment to change, which serves as a metanorm. The fifth is that the solution should be implemented and evaluated. Finally, new practices must be frozen in place and employees must be socialized into the new habits.

Open Channels of Communication. People who work together are going to talk. In order to halt decline, management needs not to stop communication, but to change the communication patterns. Replacing pessimism with optimism starts the momentum necessary for changing the outlook and expectations of employees. In addition to changing the content of informal communications, clear channels must be available for formally passing information through the organization. Quality communication is essential for stopping the decline and introducing innovations.

The process of innovation occurs within the context of interpersonal communication. One person must communicate an idea to someone else before anything is done about it. The problem is that innovative ideas are not usually discussed among people who have weak ties with one another. Albrecht and Ropp (1984) found that when two employees talked of possible innovations, they were generally peers. This is consistent with the notion that perceived homophyly plays a role in the formation of organizational relationships. "Perceived homophyly" refers to the perception that one person is similar to another in background, attitudes, and status. But it is this phenomenon that breeds groupthink and conformity in the first place. Discussions across ranks do not occur as freely as they should in any organization, and especially in one that is in decline. Uncertainty enters into the decision calculus of whether one person will risk suggesting an innovation to someone else. People are much more likely to voice ideas to someone whom they perceive to be receptive and similar to themselves, than to someone whom they perceive to be hostile, skeptical, or different. In a company already in decline, suspicion is already rampant, so this, ipso facto discourages innovative ideas from being voiced.

Some organizations socialize their members into acquiescence and punish those who offer contrary ideas. For example, Pagano and Dintino (1982) discuss the case of police forces. They believe the working milieu of the police environment has stymied the career development of many potentially good police managers. They argue that the rigid hierarchy of the paramilitary structure forces good police officers to become poor managers. Since police are socialized to be suspicious and reactive, the officer reacts to exceptions as if they were the rule. The ultimate result is that the employee who critically challenges existing policy is often branded as a deviant and a threat to the authority of the manager. Oftentimes the subliminal message is that anyone who wants to be accepted should consent to the predominant views and discourage minority views. This effectively blocks communication. Pagano and Dintino liken this to the mid-1970s fall of the Shah of Iran, whom they quote as having said: "My advisers built a wall between myself and my people. I didn't realize what was happening. When I woke up, I lost my people" (p. 30).

A Can-do Culture. Inherent to any work group are a set of norms that rule behavior. In the American setting, the desire to win is one that permeates most all groups. When management can harness this competitive urge and use it to focus the efforts of the workforce on the renewal task, energy flows into the resurrection. Another characteristic of culture that is a positive force for renewal is the desire to see things happen. Tangible rewards in a renewing organization are reinforcing.

Awareness of unspoken, unwritten norms within the organization is critical to understanding why certain actions are taken, why unusual events occur, and why people behave in certain ways. Oftentimes when an organization is in decline, management turns to an outside consultant to advise on what has gone wrong in the firm. These corporate psychiatrists do a poor job of analyzing the problem when, as outsiders, they are not privy to the values, subtleties, and informal messages circulating among "those in the know." Unfortunately, top management are excluded from the scuttlebutt on the factory floor—where actual productivity is controlled. When managers sit through endless meetings trying to secure information, they are often wasting their time, for they too are not tapping the influential messages that are never spoken in formal meetings (*The Economist*, 1984).

In terms of external communication, the organization is affected by newcomers. Sometimes a work culture will benefit from an infusion of new personnel with fresh ideas. But to make the infusion requires a trade-off. There are collective benefits to stabilized, routine, and predictable behavior. Newcomers bring adjustments to these routines. Personnel turnover and consequent adjustment to newcomers and to the values of those who remain cause internal changes (Kaufman, 1971). Employees who are often reshuffled lose the team spirit kindled through having worked together. This is a questionable trade-off to make to avoid organizational complacency (Questar, 1984). The dilemma calls for some sort of contingency planning that acknowledges and weighs the cost of complacency against the cost of rootlessness.

Constructive relationships among work groups are critical to productivity. When management attempts to introduce a change to work groups, the effects are mitigated by the preexisting relationships among the group. For example, Narayanan and Nath (1984) investigated flexitime work schedules. They found that the introduction of flexitime was well received by stable, constructive work groups. However, it made little difference in those groups that were not productive in the first place. Group cohesion is a variable that must be considered when introducing any sort of productivity improvement program. While employees in groups that lacked cohesion did not report any statistically significant change in any variable, employees in highly cohesive work groups reported improvement in flexibility, productivity, willingness to back up co-workers, and superior-subordinate relations. Change for the sake of change does not bring about improved employee morale. If things are already stable and productive, things can get better with structural change. If they are not stable and productive, structural change may not bring improvement.

The notion of firms resurrecting themselves places a simultaneous emphasis on culture, involvement, communication at all levels, and a strong consensus favoring flexibility. Organizations are social beings as long as humans are involved in them. There must be a sense of balance in the organization between the implicit and the explicit, between the needs of the individual and the needs of the organization. Given the emphasis on flexibility that a renewing organization must have, nimbleness and flexibility are essential for survival.

Up-to-date Technology. When the firm fails to incorporate innovations that are paying off in other firms, it may find itself losing out in the marketplace. Borrowing good ideas from others is a positive force that fosters renewal, but when the firm introduces technological advances the culture of the corporation is changed. Reequipping a factory often means retooling not only the skills but also the values of the workforce.

Industries as well as specific organizations are tradition bound. Socialization to the procedures, traditions, and organizational memories make change very difficult. Sometimes it is the adherence to these traditional norms which cause a firm's, or an industry's, decline. Discussing how resistant the shipping industry is to changes, Roggema and Smith (1983) attribute the reluctance to its long history, traditions, and procedures.

CASE IN POINT: THE SHIPPING INDUSTRY

Roggema and Smith studied attempts to increase crew stability, redistribute responsibility from a caste-like division between officers and seamen toward a more complex differentiation, increase flexible divisions of tasks, and decentralize management with shipboard management being in control rather than shore management. Tradition has prohibited the industry from learning new structures and styles. The recommended changes have met with severe criticism because this represents a significant departure from the traditions of the past. It is difficult to override history. The authors chide consultants who think the introduction of a few training and consulting sessions will have any lasting effect.

Adaptability. The success of some organizations relies upon their ability to change with the environment. This is particularly true of federal agencies whose emphases change with each presidential administration. Gaertner, Gaertner, and Devine (1983) examined the U.S. Environmental Protection Agency and the U.S. Mine Safety and Health Administration (MSHA) to compare their adaptibility to changes from the Carter administration to the Reagan administration. Federal organizations must simultaneously have regularized, predictable procedures and yet adapt to each administration's differing emphases. The authors contend that the Reagan transition between 1980 and 1983 produced increased centralization, less communication, and greater distrust between career and political employees. The effects were more pronounced in EPA than in MSHA because EPA's transition was more extreme. The authors contend that while private sector organizations devote efforts to the management of organizational change, the public sector efforts seem fitful and episodic. Of course this is true. Rarely would a private company the size of the EPA with interests in each state change the direction of its efforts every four years and expect to be able to function efficiently.

An organization's development efforts are not interchangeable parts that may be applied to any organization regardless of its corporate culture. Tainio and Santalainen (1984) compared American organizations' development efforts in foreign companies. American values are embodied in the managerial grid and other techniques that are designed to produce tangible differences quickly in American firms. Tainio and Santalainen say the managerial grid does not work in Finland because Finns are more egalitarian, exhibit less "machismo," are more skeptical of ambition, and are more socially responsible than Americans. The managerial grid reinforces concern for people and concern for production, producing a "one best way manager." This represents a keen respect for an individual's personal development and produces visible but short-term gains. Often these short-term results occur without producing deeper organizational impacts, however.

Many actions are likely to produce a visible short-term change, but a long-term change will only result from several concurrent interventions, including those that affect managerial, organizational, and technological operations. While short-term gains are essential to reinforce the effort required in the renewal process, long-term gains must be produced to bring about wide-ranging organizational renewal.

In terms of change, per se, Ramaprasad (1982) emphasizes the necessity of double loop learning in place of single loop. Single loop learning relies upon current norms and constraints and results in incremental alterations, which will not lead to revolutionary change. Double loop learning changes the norms of the system. It involves attending to positive as well as negative feedback. Organizations need negative feedback loops to maintain themselves within tolerable limits of a steady state and they need positive feedback loops to move from one steady state to another. In other words, the firm must be attentive to both positive and negative feedback so that it can bring itself to a steady state.

Reorganization or Merger. Even the case of filing for bankruptcy serves as a force for renewal. The filing makes obvious what had been previously undiscussable; thus, it opens communication. Bankruptcy has the power to give life to dying companies. It forces creditors and owners to settle previous obligations and reorganize the firm into a healthier enterprise. Half of the firms that file under Chapter XI of the Bankruptcy Code succeed after reorganizing (Giroux & Wiggins, Jr., 1983).

Reorganization results in one of three events: successful reorganization, merger, or liquidation. There are preexisting characteristics that contribute to a company's being able to successfully reorganize versus those that liquidate. Bankruptcy is only a single event in the failure process. For example, both Interstate Stores' and W. T. Grants' financial troubles began as early as a decade before they both declared Chapter XI bankruptcy in the mid-1970s. Both operated large discount store chains. A U.S. Bankruptcy Court ordered Grant to liquidate its assets four months after it had filed. Unlike Grant, Interstate Stores successfully reorganized and emerged from bankruptcy as Toys "R" Us, a successful toy retailer. The outcome of bankruptcy differed significantly for these two companies. One reorganized and resurrected itself; one did not (Giroux & Wiggins, Jr., 1983).

There is a continuum of events from bad to worst in terms of business problems. Going from least to worst these events are (1) operating results below expectations; (2) nonpayment of dividends; (3) net loss and negative cash flow trends; (4) lowered bond rating; (5) deteriorating operation results year after year; (6) debt accommodations; (7) load default bankruptcy; and finally (8) liquidation. For the first three, the alternatives available to the firm are policy changes and operating reorganizations. For the last five, the only solution is reorganization. Alternatives for the severe side of the continuum are also discontinued operations, merger with a solvent corporation, or bankruptcy petition.

An organization dies when it ceases to carry out the routine actions that sustain its structure, its flow of resources, and the allegiance of its members. Newer organizations are more likely to die than older ones and the type of technology or industry influences the type of demise. Merger is an alternative that may or may not be a force for renewal. Freeman, Carroll, and Hannan (1983) correlate the age of organizations with their death rates and their proclivity to merge rather than liquidate. Comparing labor unions and newspaper publishing companies, the authors conclude that there is a liability of youth in both of these industries, but the liability differs according to whether death will come by dissolution or by absorption through merger. Newspapers are more likely to dissolve, while labor unions are more likely to merge with other unions. As a matter of fact, the International Brotherhood of Teamsters rejoined the AFL-CIO in October 1986, following thirty years of being an independent union. The merger strengthened both the weakening AFL-CIO as well as the Teamsters Union (Bernstein & Garland, 1987; Spector, 1987).

What does all this say about forces for renewal? Organizational goals focus the energy of the organization in a unified effort. Management experience is a positive force that controls the direction a firm takes in its renewal efforts. Communication is critical to resurrection and the content of messages sent has a direct impact on the morale of the work-force. Cultural norms that favor winning serve as an energizer in the renewal process. The drive to "keep up with the Joneses" can be harnessed to successfully introduce new technology and productivity standards. The urge to "make things better" marks a readiness for constructive organizational change. Bankruptcy or merger represent a second chance for the organization to pull itself up by its bootstraps.

External forces generate resurrection as well as internal forces, but to some extent the former differ in nature. Usually a more accurate statement is that different levels within the organization face different environments and one of those faced is the external one. Within the hierarchy, the top level faces the external environment, while the middle level faces an internal milieu of upper management and lower level employees. Lower levels face the day-to-day issues of the task at hand. An organization must be responsive to all its environments in order to thrive. Unresponsiveness is an organizational killer. Scott (1981) emphasizes the importance of acknowledging these plural environments and suggests that the natural selection process results in the death of those firms that are not responsive. The converse is that responsiveness to the environment is essential for organizational renewal.

RENEWAL STRATEGIES THAT FAIL

Regardless of the forces being generated within the organization and external to it, and the fact that there is no one best way to revive a declining firm, there are some activities that are doomed to fail. For example, some firms fall into a planning trap. Although a well structured planning cycle, system, and manual have been developed, they may address the wrong questions, rely on the wrong structure to produce meaningful answers, or rely on the actions of people who are not fully committed to them. In addition to the planning trap, there is also the "lack-of-focus trap" (Horovitz, 1984). In this instance a strategy is formulated but the focus is vague. The battlefields have not been delineated within the organization to correspond to the market battlefield. This is what happens when management decides to change one unit of an organization because it is changeable and avoid not changing an intractable unit, even though the intractable unit is the problem. The problem is not brought into focus before the solution is put in place.

Another doomed strategy is the shotgun approach. This happens when people feel desperate, think something must be done, and done now, and so take action in numerous ways without a thoughtful plan. Since usually inappropriate action results, energy is diverted away from the real source of the problem and disrupts units that were not part of the problem in the first place.

Another problem that is difficult but essential to address is secrecy. People are embarrassed to acknowledge that the organization with which they are involved is in trouble. For very personal reasons, top management often tries to "keep a lid on" the problem. But by doing this, it promotes a poor exploration of alternatives and keeps the decline undiscussable. Self-protection and defensiveness take over and people in one unit point fingers and place blame on others.

Doing something to deal with the decline, and doing it very energetically may still not produce the resurrection. The "do it, because we've got to do something'' may be as wasteful of effort as not doing anything. Expending energy on fruitless tasks is activity that feeds on itself but does not produce a desired change in the problem. It is not worthwhile and will not produce the desired resurrection unless the activity serves a symbolic function of making people aware that there is a problem. Attempting to resurrect a firm that is suffering from a lack of resources requires more resources, but pouring money into a declining firm is unwise until a well planned strategy is developed for budgeting the resources in the most productive manner.

Making one set of changes in one unit or area without making another set of changes in another unit or area is useless. For example, administrative changes and technological changes typically go hand in hand and to turn a declining firm around, it is necessary to make changes in both rather than in only one. Doing one without the other is not sufficient. Technical innovations are a means of changing and improving the performance of the technical system of an organization. Administrative innovations deal with the social system, such as the implementation of a new way to recruit personnel or allocate resources and to structure tasks, authority, and rewards. It includes innovations in organizational structure and in the management of people. Technical innovations are more observable and are perceived to be relatively more advantageous than administrative innovations. However, administrative innovations are more complex than technical innovations to implement. Any change in the technical system of an organization sets certain constraints and requirements for the social system.

Damanpour and Evan (1984) think that the introduction of administrative innovations has a greater impact on the overall performance of an organization than the introduction of technical innovations. Administrative innovations can change an organization's climate, communication patterns, interdepartmental relations, and personnel policies. After studying eighty-five public libraries, the authors conclude that libraries adopt technical innovations at a faster rate than administrative innovations, but the adoption of administrative innovations tends to trigger the adoption of technical innovations more readily than the reverse. Those libraries that adopt administrative innovations have a greater payoff in the end, because the administrative changes pave the way for bringing in technological changes.

SUMMARY

Organizations pass through undulating waves of pressures and cross-pressures during their evolutions. When they fail to keep abreast of these, decline sets in. A proactive stance by management is the best prescription for dealing early with decline. Timing and leadership are critical for bringing the problem to people's awareness and instituting corrective measures. There are numerous forces that can be harnessed to resurrect a firm.

Resurrection is characterized by several distinct and well executed movements: responsiveness to plural environments, inculcation of metanorms that provide the work force with the vision and faith to proceed with the resurrection, communication throughout the organization, and administrative and technological improvements.

• *Responsiveness.* The organization is beset by numerous environmental forces, each producing different pushes and pulls. The internal environment denotes those forces within the firm, while the external environment denotes those pushes and pulls exerting influence from the outside. The organization in decline has succumbed to some forces at the expense of others. Responsiveness requires an awareness of which forces are critical and must be acted upon at once.

• *Metanorms.* A company's culture must have within it a set of metanorms that rise above the usual norms dictating routine work behavior and procedures. Metanorms prescribe intangible behavior such as an optimism that the organization can and will thrive again. It is these overarching beliefs that will hold the workforce together while they institute the many changes. The metanorm of everyone working together toward a greater good characterizes the successful Japanese firm and is something that Ouchi (1981) touts in Theory Z firms. It can be useful as well for resurrecting troubled firms.

• *Communication.* Open communication must be fostered. Communication is going to occur through the employee grapevine as well as through formal channels. When there is an atmosphere of secrecy, the secrecy itself will be talked about if there is no substance to discuss.

• *Administrative and Technological Improvement.* These two categories of changes go hand in hand—one affecting the other, and one often dictating the other. It is not enough to bring in machines that will do the job better. Changes in people must also be made so that the human machinery is in place to capitalize on the technological changes.

6

Stages of Renewal

Although the end results are different, organizational resurrection and organizational decline are similar in their progression. Both occur in stages and each stage builds on the foundation provided by the prior stage. The resurrection process is characterized by a series of steps resembling an ascending staircase. Each step up represents a new phase grounded in the prior phase. Between each phase is a plateau.

There is a critical difference between the process of resurrection and the process of decline. Once decline is set in motion, it tends to stay in motion until purposely stopped. No inherent forces keep revitalization in motion, however. What gravitational forces there are work against ascending the staircase.

The ascending-the-staircase analogy represents processes similar to the unfreezing of old habits and refreezing of new habits necessary in organizational development strategies. To move upward unproductive but comfortable routines are changed, habits altered, objectives clearly specified, and perspectives changed. Day-to-day work activities are transformed into deliberate confrontations with the usual and customary way of doing business.

There are at least seven elements involved in revitalizing the firm: skilled, committed management; carefully managed assets; reasoned risk taking; development of a clear corporate strategy; careful selection of the target market; familiarity with markets and consumers; and capitalizing on luck and timing (Norman, 1985). Revitalization occurs one step at a time in carefully planned, strategically timed, and thoroughly monitored increments. Figure 4 illustrates the stages involved in this process.

Figure 4
Structure of the Resurrection Process

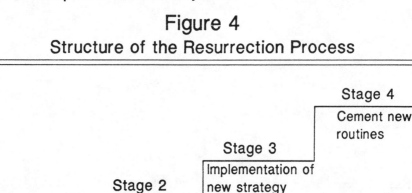

Decision & Commitment from the Top. Stage 1 represents a commitment at the apex of the organization to whatever changes are necessary. This implies a willful determination to turn the organization around and is the critical foundation for all further revitalization efforts. Without commitment at this level, the implementation of new strategies may get started but seldom becomes widely accepted and institutionalized.

Strategy & Consensus Building. Stage 2 represents the development of a clearly planned strategy with which all significant actors in the organization are in accord. This stage represents the beginning of pervasive behavioral and cultural change. Essential at this stage is an infusion of commitment, energy, and direction to complement any infusion of funds and technology. Widespread consensus develops in this phase and generates support for changes about to come.

Those who function as the trend setters of the organization shape the opinions of those around them. In Stage 2 it is critical for these opinion shapers to "buy in" to the revitalization strategy so that they will communicate their agreement to those around them. Unintended consequences occur when changes are put in place that reallocate power and influence among employees. Those who stand to lose power or status will become obstacles to the revitalization effort unless they are firmly committed early in the process and understand the actions being taken.

Implementation of New Strategy. Stage 3 is the phase during which implementation takes place and overt change occurs. Decisive actions are taken and efficient resource utilization becomes the focus of attention. Everyone in the firm gets the word that things are on the move, changes are being made, and the turnaround is underway. The organization stays in this phase long enough that everyone becomes accustomed to the new order of the day.

Cementing New Routines. Stage 4 represents the institutionalization of successful strategies. It is in this stage that the new way of doing things freezes into place and becomes a part of the culture. By the time Stage 4 is reached, new strategies have been implemented and new procedures are becoming comfortable routines. The approaches to work, the habits, and the litanies become a part of the culture. This phase can only be put into play if all the preceding stages have been successfully completed

Plateaus. The staircase pattern of Stages 1, 2, 3, and 4 simulates an ecological approach to resurrection, with each stage giving rise to the next. One set of changes within the organization generates the next set. Between each pair of stages is a plateau. Each plateau represents the time required to digest the changes that occurred in the prior stage and become accustomed to the newness. Moving too rapidly from one stage to another prevents this cementing action from taking place. The upward climb has much less momentum than the downward spiral and plateaus provide breathing space before the next hurdle arrives. During this time, routines are established that make the new behaviors part of a usual workday. Plateaus are different from setbacks. Plateaus are essential phases of revitalization, while setbacks diminish the progress made during the most recent step up.

The plateau between the first stage, decision and commitment, and strategy and consensus, is a quiet one of idea generation and momentum building. It is also by necessity the shortest plateau. Too long a time at the plateau without moving upward is tantamount to slipping backward into decline. No actual visible action in the resurrection has been taken yet. It is at this time that the top managerial staff becomes committed to the realities of what it will take to revive the firm. The operatives within the organization may have sensed the new commitment but they will not yet feel its effects.

The plateau between strategy and consensus, and implementation may be of slightly longer duration than the first plateau. It is the time when everyone in the firm must become committed to the changes that are about to be put in motion. In the second stage, strategy and consensus, a plan is developed for resurrecting the firm. Consensus is reached by those who shape opinions in the organization and news filters throughout the firm through formal channels and through the grapevine. Clarity of the goal is paramount, as is clarity of the message. It is during this plateau that purging takes place. It is necessary that those who do not agree with the strategy leave the firm to prevent their sabotaging the new commitment.

The final plateau is between the implementation stage and the cementing stage. This is by necessity the longest of the plateaus. Here new procedures must become habits. New routines must be developed so that what was new in the resurrection strategy is now commonplace. It takes time for the new to become the norm. Somewhere during this phase employees will slip back into what they know best—routines they used to follow. This plateau is used for extinguishing the memories of the old routines and replacing them with the new.

Revitalization requires innovations in the technological, environmental, organizational, and human domains (McGinnis & Ackelsberg, 1983). Figure 5 illustrates this point. The technological domain involves advances in machines, electronics, or production and service delivery. The environmental domain includes capitalizing on market trends, community preferences, and other external factors such as economic, regulatory, or political forces. It also involves the interface between the environment and the organization. The organizational domain includes the chain of command; reporting structure; enforcement of policies, procedures, and standards; and superordinate goals. The human domain includes individual acceptance of innovations, interpersonal skills, employee motivation, work skills, energy, persistence, achievement orientation, and sense of timing. An examination of the attention focused on each domain helps to clarify the structure and function of each stage of renewal.

Figure 5
Domains of Revitalization

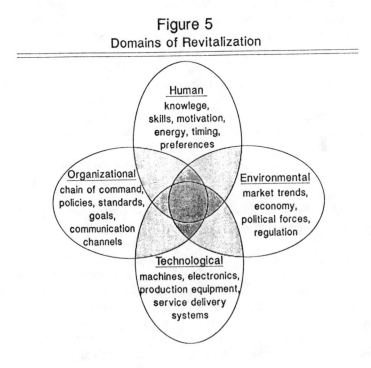

Human
knowlege,
skills, motivation,
energy, timing,
preferences

Organizational
chain of command,
policies, standards,
goals,
communication
channels

Environmental
market trends,
economy,
political forces,
regulation

Technological
machines, electronics,
production equipment,
service delivery
systems

STAGE 1—DECISION AND COMMITMENT FROM THE TOP

Central to Stage 1 is a mix of the human, organizational, and environmental domains. Technological considerations are not essential until strategy has been mapped out in the second stage.

Human Domain. Those at the helm are the ones who have to decide whether to pull the plug or breathe life into the ailing firm. The first stage of renewal is accomplished when top management determines and communicates an earnest commitment to turn around the organization. Halfhearted commitment or only lip service to revitalization does not provide the energy needed to convince everyone that the task can be achieved or is even worth attempting. Many at levels lower than the CEO may be fully committed to the turnaround, but sooner or later their actions will fail to produce results without the support and impetus from the top. Likewise the introduction of sophisticated technology is not sufficient to signal renewal. It may symbolize it, but it is the people at the apex of the company who will be the driving force to make or break the renewal.

CASE IN POINT: EASTERN AIR LINES

Under Frank Borman's leadership Eastern Air Lines suffered rather than gained from the 1978 airline deregulation policy. For example, Borman used obfuscation when explaining Eastern's abysmal 1983 performance. His tone was not that of a CEO breathing life into Eastern Airlines. He explained: "Relentless increases in operating expenses plus continued heavy competition that restricted traffic growth and fare relief, severely impacted Eastern in 1983." A writer translating Borman's words gave them this form: "We lost $183.7 million in 1983" (Moskowitz, 1984). Short, but not sweet. Obfuscation rarely does much to instill confidence. By 1986 Eastern had succumbed to a buy out offer from Texas Air and Borman had resigned (*Business Week*, 1986a; Shifrin, 1986). After the deal was struck Borman was more direct: "Capitalism without bankruptcy is like Christianity without hell" (*Fortune*, 1986a).

Frank Lorenzo took over when Borman left. Lorenzo's attitude about deregulation was upbeat. Speaking of the effect of airline deregulation, he said: "Ten years ago we had an industry where you never could make much money. Now the upside opportunities are vastly improved. But deregulation also provided an opportunity for airlines to fail" (*Fortune*, 1986b). Lorenzo foresees the formation of what he terms "megalines" within the industry. Tracing the trends of the airline industry since deregulation, he says the industry has gone through the new airline phase into the consolidation and cost-cutting phase, and will soon find itself into the megaline phase, in which the United States will be served by five to eight major carriers instead of the number existing in the mid-1980s (Engardio, 1987).

Turning a company around means convincing everyone that the "business as usual" attitude is a thing of the past. Finkin (1985) argues that to start, the CEO has to excite the dispirited organization. Otherwise, staff sit back and await developments. Workers have to be jolted out of their passive stance. Finkin urges an awakening process in which the CEO picks the 20 percent of the elements that contribute to 80 percent of the problems. Step forward, he says, and make bold, decisive, significant improvements. When this has been accomplished, the chain reaction has begun. Then streamline the organization, getting rid of those who are unproductive, and form a lean team that believes in its ability to make things happen.

CASE IN POINT: PORT OF ALBANY

It is not unusual that one person is given credit for the turnaround of an entire organization. The case of M. Elizabeth Reddish and the Port of Albany is an example. Reddish is credited with having turned around the Port of Albany. In 1985 it went from being financially strapped into being a moneymaker for the first time in its fifty-year history. Reddish is given credit for having led the port through a massive renewal project and seeing to it that it carved a regional economic niche in the face of a rapidly changing shipping industry. Prior to Reddish's intervention the port was running annual deficits of $300,000 to $400,000. The docks and facilities were crumbling and the port had a reputation for punctuated violent labor trouble and illicit drug activity. Under Reddish's leadership, the port established new rent schedules, increased user fees, opened projects to competitive bid, and spearheaded a bond issue drive that produced funds for a face lift to the facilities. After the improvements port management had the luxury of focusing its attention on expanding port-based operations and jobs (Dopp, 1986).

Organizational Domain. Strategic advantage comes from changing the way a company behaves. It is less top management's role to identify and solve problems than to create an organization that can identify and solve its own problems (Hayes, 1985). To do this requires a clear vision of where the organization is headed and the strength to steer it there. Clarity of vision is the greatest influence on any company's culture (Ackerman, 1984; Truskie, 1984; Bhide, 1986). Clarity refers to an organization's ability to define and communicate its raison d'etre. This provides a blueprint for targeting initiatives, designating objectives, and setting performance standards. Lane Kirkland's comments about the need for the AFL-CIO to renew itself provides an example.

CASE IN POINT: AFL-CIO

In 1985 Lane Kirkland, AFL-CIO President, was attempting to resurrect the federation. He likened the organization to one over which vultures were circling, but one which, at the same time, was on the threshold of resurgence. He was trying to polish the AFL-CIO's battered image and modernize the union message. (The number of union members had dropped from 20.1 million to 17.4 million since 1980, which was a loss of 13 percent at a time when the civilian workforce was expanding by 5 percent.) He started the revival by admitting that unions themselves are to blame for the thirty-year decline in membership (Gay, 1985). Kirkland then had to develop, communicate, and maintain a clear vision of where the organization needed to go, of what it must become, and where the most predictable potholes would lurk.

Clarity provides guidance to personnel so that management's actions do not seem mysterious. When workers share a vision with those at the top, they have a clearer understanding of corporate goals and strategy. An absence of clarity results in excessively complex strategies that are difficult to track and too ambiguous to evaluate meaningfully.

Identity influences many dimensions of the business enterprise: how it is organized, what behaviors are expected of people, the kinds of people it hires, and how strategies are developed and implemented. A "Marlboro Man" identity means that the culture will reward rugged individualism and risk taking. A "team player" identity means that the culture rewards those who are loyal to the group and supportive of one another. Other organizations identify themselves according to the person at the top, and the culture then reinforces deference to that one person. Some organizations identify themselves with a segment of the work force. For example, the National Aeronautics and Space Administration publicly identifies itself not with the thousands of engineers and scientists it employs, nor with its administrator, but with its small but elite astronaut corps.

A realistic clarity of vision paves the way for critically assessing the organization's success markers: productivity, profitability, turnaround time, and market share. Even in the first few stumbling steps of renewal, people have to stop justifying failure and start looking for better ways to do things and better ways that work (Brown & Elvers, 1983). Maintaining the status quo in a declining organization offers no reward. An organization has to be ready to change its basic approach, regardless of how fearful the unknown is.

Stage 1 must generate a sense of optimistic positivism manifested in the belief that individual and group action will pay off. A problem that companies confront in this initial stage is the discouraged, "can't do" frame of mind. Complacency and "can't do" attitudes have to be purged before the revitalization can get underway (Marwood, 1985). A "can do" litany helps provide the momentum necessary to energize those who are not quite convinced that the organization's future is optimistic enough to warrant spending their time and energy on it. But it is not enough to leap blindly forward into optimism. The optimism must be the product of a realistic appraisal.

Environmental Domain. It is not sufficient to focus effort only on the milieu within the organization. The public has to be dealt with directly because once the external environment believes in a company's future, it is easier for all those within the company to believe in it. On the other hand, once the public has decided the company is in trouble, customers disappear and it does have trouble, whether or not the original perception was correct. A hostile public generates a hostile media. The media sensationalize the organization's problems, people read and then talk about the problems, the media report on them some more, and a vicious cycle of negativism erupts. An organization on the rebound is helped immeasurably by its leaders being in the public eye convincing them the turnaround is underway. For example, when Samuel Armacost stepped down as CEO of troubled BankAmerica in 1986, he did so to help deal with the negative perceptions among the public. He said he was stepping down because it was in "the best interests of our shareholders, customers and employees" (United Press International, 1986a).

STAGE 2—STRATEGY AND CONSENSUS BUILDING

The human, organizational, and environmental domains are central to Stage 2 as they are in Stage 1. The difference between the two stages is the scope of concern. In Stage 1 the scope is limited to those at the apex of the hierarchy. Stage 2 reaches further, involving personnel and considerations at all ranks. This is the stage for a thorough identification of problems followed by a clearly articulated strategy for solving them. Strategy is situational, according not only to industry, but to the specific configuration of the culture of the organization. After the commitment has been made at the top level of the organization, new operating plans for accomplishing the resurrection come into play. These include strategies for quality enhancement, marketing, public relations, and productivity (Heany, 1985). This is the stage at which reasoned risk taking enters the picture. Samuel Armacost, CEO of BankAmerica from 1980 to 1986, risked and lost.

CASE IN POINT: BANKAMERICA CORPORATION

BankAmerica is a large banking corporation struggling to make a turnaround. In October 1986, it reported assets of $117 billion but had accumulated $1 billion in losses over the five previous quarters. It had been ill-prepared for deregulation of the banking industry and the economic downswings of the 1980s. Samuel Armacost, its CEO from 1980 to 1986, had attempted to overhaul the corporation. Interviewed midway through his tenure as CEO, he said the culture of BankAmerica had been one that sanctioned size and doing things by the book, regardless of the customer's needs. Armacost said that the tough part of his job derived from the corporation's desire to sit back and let him make all the decisions in the turbulence of a deregulated environment. He felt he could not afford to do that because it would not develop staff's capabilities and he, by himself, could not create the momentum necessary to correct the organization's problems. Instead he tried to develop an innovative entrepreneurial approach (Hector, 1985). In the first quarter of 1981 the corporation reported a 19 percent decline in profit. In January 1985 the bank disclosed mortgage fraud costing $95 million. It reported a $337 million loss for 1985. In September 1985, the bank sold its headquarters building in San Francisco for $660 million to raise cash and accelerated layoffs of employees. Armacost is credited with having pared some of BankAmerica's operations and embarked on an aggressive advertising program for its retail operations. However, Armacost repeatedly forecast improvements in the bank's operations, only to later announce huge losses (United Press International, 1986a). When Armacost stepped down, his predecessor, A. W. Clausen, who had named Armacost to succeed him in 1980, stepped back in to replace him

(*Time*, 1986). Analysts following the jaded attempts to resurrect BankAmerica feared that the corporation had taken a step backward by reappointing the former CEO (Pauly with Lubenow & Reese, 1986, p. 56).

Organizational Domain. Organizations may be categorized by their strategies as prospectors, analyzers, defenders, or reactors. Prospectors are those that are first with a new idea. They are true innovators with creative ideas and because they are first they have the edge on competition. Analyzers are those that sit back and wait to see how the prospectors do before they dive in. Analyzers are able to learn from mistakes of the prospectors but they do not have the first mover advantage. Defenders are those that hold the line and protect what they have from encroachment or loss. Reactors are those that do not fall neatly into one of the previous categories. They react sometimes differently to different ideas and markets, depending on the environment. The optimal strategic approach depends on the mix of market opportunities, habits and traditions of the company, level of competition, expertise, and opportunity costs.

Strategies are either corporate or business. Corporate strategy asks the question "what business are we in?" while business strategy asks the question "how shall we compete in each business?" (Chaffee, 1985). Whether a strategy is corporate or business, it focuses on the organization as a whole and may be of three types: linear, adaptive, or interpretive. In a linear strategy, planning is methodical, directed, and sequential. This strategy requires that the organization be tightly coupled, so that all decisions made at the top can be communicated and implemented throughout the organization. With an adaptive strategy, an organization has to continually assess external and internal conditions in order to adapt to them. Monitoring the environment and making changes are simultaneous and continuous functions in the adaptive model. With the interpretive strategy, frames of reference of stakeholders in the organization must be monitored and oriented. This allows the organization and its environment to be understood by one another.

The turnaround of Chrysler Corporation resulted from a combination of strategies (Hampton, 1987; Hampton with Rossant, 1987). The list that Iacocca sets forth in this Case in Point shows a blending of linear and adaptive strategies.

CASE IN POINT: CHRYSLER CORPORATION REVISITED

Lee Iacocca (1983) outlined the six steps Chrysler took to turn itself around:

1. It reduced salaried positions from 160,000 to 80,000, thus creating a leaner team.
2. It reduced fixed costs by about $2 billion. It closed or consolidated twenty obsolete and outmoded plants and modernized the remaining forty plants to make them among the most efficient and productive in the industry.
3. It simplified operations by reducing the number of different parts in its manufacturing system by one-third, and thus cut its inventory by $1 billion.
4. It launched a concerted effort to improve the quality of both its finished products and the components that go into them.
5. It restructured its balance sheet and retired its U.S. bank debt.
6. It embarked on a five-year $6.6 billion product program. By 1983 Chrysler was half the size but twice the company it had been in 1980. That is a turnaround.

Strategic planning, for its own sake, is shortsighted in some respects. Too many times the abstractions that fill the plans are out of touch with reality or too finite to convey the information needed. Too much emphasis on numerical measurement fails to be an impetus to a turnaround because numbers do not capture the essence of the future and do not acknowledge the different perspectives from the different levels in the organization. Each level has concerns that differ from those at other levels (Slevin and Pinto, 1987).

Arguing against a cut-and-dried approach to strategic planning, Hayes (1985) argues for a clear direction to travel but believes that the means for getting there should be left to whomever is traveling the path. As an analogy, he says that if one is lost on a highway, a road map is very useful. However, when lost in a swamp, the road map is useless. What is most helpful then is a compass that will indicate the general direction to be taken. He argues that supplying personnel with a compass is more productive than supplying them with a map because it keeps everyone responsible for the organization's prosperity.

Success rests on the ability to exploit opportunities as they arise, where they arise. Goals and objectives set at one level of the organization may be meaningless to those at other levels. Objectives that have little meaning for large segments of an organization cannot be shared and do not weld it together. Like return on investment, goals have meaning and value for senior managers who understand the need to allocate capital efficiently and who are themselves evaluated on their ability to do so. However, return on investment has almost no meaning for production workers whose only contact with investment decisions is indirect: roofs that leak, old equipment that breaks down, new equipment that creates more problems than it solves. What does have meaning for these workers is getting the work done correctly, meeting delivery schedules, and the satisfaction that comes from doing a good job as part of an appreciative organization.

Human Domain. The opinion shapers have to feel committed to the resurrection. Because numbers do not convey the human dimension, quantitative tools for decision making are not necessarily tools of renewal. Motivation, group dynamics, and interpersonal communication play significant roles in the revitalization process (Ledford & Lawler, 1982). The development of shared, constructive values serves several functions: as a general guide to decision making, as a framework for making sense of personal experience, as an influence on the level of cooperation, and as an influence on the degree to which employees identify with the organization. Projects are more likely to thrive when workers and lower level managers participate in developing them through suggestion programs, quality circles, and identifying the company's long-term success with their own personal success. Innovations and intrapreneurship from below cannot be ordered. It develops voluntarily.

CASE IN POINT: TEXAS INSTRUMENTS

The right kind of leadership is critical to accomplish the tasks involved in revitalization. Texas Instruments has gone through a change of CEO's in its attempt to revitalize. In May 1985, Jerry Junkins, a twenty-seven-year Texas Instruments veteran widely regarded as a sound, likable manager was named CEO. The former leadership was blamed for promoting an air of suspicion, mistrust, and cool distance. As the new CEO, Junkins stepped up to his position and immediately started spending much of his time listening to employees. He felt the prior air of suspicion stifled risk taking and contributed to TI's troubles (O'Reilly, 1985). By the end of 1986, Texas Instruments was making a no-holds-barred run to hold onto the semiconductor market. It introduced the world's first four-megabit chip, a supersophisticated semiconductor capable of storing more than four million bits of information on a wafer the size of a child's fingernail (Koepp, 1986).

Although there are various successful strategies for revitalizing a comatose organization, there is one sure-fire way to fail. Innovations, regardless of their brilliance, that do not fit together and contribute to each other are a waste of energy. Poorly considered strategies applied indiscriminately to a set of problems is ineffective. Innovations must be compatible with the organization, fit with the technological system, fit with skills and training, fit with organizational and work patterns, fit with industrial relations patterns, and fit with the culture (Kiechel III, 1982; Seeger, 1984).

There are three dimensions to the CEO's role in an organization undergoing revitalization: expecter, appreciator, and risk absorber (Brown & Kay, 1985). As expecter, the CEO must expect innovation to take place. As appreciator, the CEO expresses appreciation of innovation both verbally and monetarily. As risk absorber, the CEO absorbs the cost when the innovations fail. This frees the mid-level manager to be the intrapreneur. First-line supervisors often catch the blame for productivity problems because the most obvious problems are manifested at the operating level. Although manifested at that level, problems may have been brought about by policies instituted at higher levels.

It is tempting for management to succumb to the Good Fairy Syndrome, believing that problems will be solved when a good fairy appears and waves a magic wand (Hays, 1985). Good organization fairies are often trendy interventions such as Transactional Analysis, sensitivity groups, the Boston Consulting Group's growth/share matrix, and organization development attempts that are applied once rather than repeatedly over time. Good fairies typically fail to produce results after the initial enthusiasm for them wanes.

Only a consistent, ongoing program addressing the continuing management development needs of the organization makes a lasting contribution to overall managerial effectiveness. Techniques accepted and put into practice by supervisors must be supported by the organization where the supervisors work. If they are not reinforced in the day-to-day managerial situation, then even the best training programs do not significantly improve effectiveness.

Having timely, clear communication with all segments of the organization is essential to the revitalization strategy. All relevant groups at all levels in the organization must be represented in any strategy formulation process. For effective communication to and from these groups, monitoring and feedback must be in place, along with foresight into the likely change in the balance of interests. In his book *Corporate Communications* (1984) William Ruch says communications are the unseen infrastructure of the organization. Listing numerous methods of upward and downward communication, Ruch says top management personnel need to be more creative in opening lines of communication. Rather than giving just the good news, communicating both bad news and good news maintains credibility with employees and quells unfounded rumors. Because of the problems and obstacles to a free flow of information, Ruch reports that while 64 percent of employees prefer to receive information from their own supervisors, and only 6 percent prefer to receive it from the grapevine, the fact of the matter is that 78 percent receive current information from the grapevine. The lifeblood of an organizational turnaround is its ability to move information and ideas from the bottom to the top and back down again in a continuous dialogue (Rosenberg & Schewe, 1985). Modes of communicating vary in their degree of sophistication. There are channels as elementary as bulletin boards hanging by water fountains to channels as sophisticated as desktop on-line electronic bulletin boards.

CASE IN POINT: SOUTHERN COMPANY SERVICES

Southern Company Services uses the office bulletin board as an inexpensive, readily accessible medium:

A survey of 90 percent of the 3,000 employees of Southern Company Services of Atlanta, Georgia, found that its information boards rank second only to the company's monthly publication in readership and credibility among employees. Topics on company boards range from electric utility industry-related business and company news to feature stories and health tips. . . . News and cartoons are changed daily at the company's 43 boards; other items remain on them from two days to a week. When major events occur in a business day, they are posted as a "Flash" or a "Bulletin." (Ruch, 1984, p. 139)

Focusing on culture and communication, Ouchi (1982) emphasizes the importance of a firm adopting a Theory Z culture. He says there are seven elements to such a firm: long-term employment, slow evaluation and promotion, nonspecialized career paths, consensus decision making, collective responsibility, distinctive management philosophy, and holistic relations. Ouchi's argument is that such a culture creates conditions under which an atmosphere of trust will develop. Freed from the animosities and jealousies inherent in individualist cultures, each person is more likely to work together in pursuing the organization's goals. In Ouchi's words, making everybody part of the strategic information stream of the business is critical because it makes everybody an owner. "People who are part of the team, who "own" the company and "own" their job, regularly perform a thousand percent better than the rest'' (p. 26). There must be trust among employees that information they are receiving is accurate and trust that they are seen as worthy human beings with something to contribute to the organization.

There is more to the picture than what Ouchi outlines. America's federal civil service has been marked by guaranteed tenure and slow promotion since passage of the Pendleton Act in 1883. But Americans are not satisfied with either the efficiency or productivity of federal agencies. The strategy has to fit the organization's external as well as internal culture. In a competitive, individualist culture such as that from which the U.S. work force derives, guaranteed tenure works to the detriment of productivity. People schooled in the Horatio Alger myth that hard work will lead to bigger and better tangible rewards do not respond well to the lack of a tangible reward in terms of heightened pay or speedy promotions.

Managers must be credible to those whom they supervise. Mendleson and Golen (1985) say that there are three critical elements to this perception: expertness, relatedness, and trustworthiness. Expertness means that the managers are skilled. Relatedness refers to a sense that the manager relates to employees in a respecting, trusting fashion. Trustworthiness means that the supervised feel comfortable trusting the supervisor.

The ambience must be right for revitalization to progress from a desire to a reality. Citing what he called the ten best managed factories, Bylinsky (1984) selected those that were tops in their industries in either productivity or product quality or both. At these ten best, managers and workers worked as a team rather than as adversaries. He said that workers got so caught up in the effort to do a good job that at the best plants—Lincoln Electric, for example—machinists had been known to make their own tools to do their work better.

Environmental Domain. As critical as the organizational and human domains are to Stage 2, the external environment cannot be ignored. Organizations trying to revitalize themselves must take note of the changes taking place within the external environment and translate these into plans for future action (Zammuto, 1985). They must also develop and implement strategies that are consistent with the underlying nature of the decline occurring. When an organization responds to environmental changes early, errors can be tolerated because the organization is still operating in a relatively munificent environment. When the firm is already in a crisis, errors become fatal. Past successes may have resulted in a detachment from current environmental realities. While assumptions on which successful past actions were based have become embedded in an organization, assumptions that were once correct may be invalidated by changing environmental conditions.

The petrochemical industry is especially affected by uncontrollable environmental circumstances. Monsanto, for example, has had to adjust to the volatile market. In the early 1980s it lost over $300 million on old line businesses, with fibers and styrene proving the worst performers. Monsanto people went into culture shock because they had become accustomed to the halcyon days of the petrochemical industry. Now they are revamping their strategy and are becoming a risk-taking outfit gambling on research that will not pay off until the 1990s, if it pays off at all (Labich, 1984). The downturn in the petrochemical industry is taking its toll on other companies as well. In 1984 Texaco, Atlantic Richfield, and Mobil Oil Company chalked up extraordinarily low returns on equity and Mobil's earnings continued to fall in 1985 (Nulty, 1985; *National Petroleum News*, 1987).

Quaker is a corporation that has wrangled with its external environment but is succeeding. In the 1970s and early 1980s it responded to customer interest in granola bars and successfully competed with General Mills, the early leader of the granola bar market. By 1985 Quaker had become the leader (McComas, 1985). It also had to respond to the decline in the birth rate. In 1969 Quaker had acquired Fisher-Price toys, making it heavily dependent on toddlers for its market. As the baby boomers came of age, it was forced to design toys for older children. In 1984 Fisher-Price introduced eight new toys for older kids in its audio-visual line: children's versions of grownups' stereos, cameras, and tape recorders.

Quality and customer satisfaction are critical to organizational turn-arounds. Peters and Austin (1985) emphasize finding out what the customer wants and producing it in the form of a quality product. Successful product innovation and customer service are built not only on a bedrock of listening to the market but of reading between the lines to find what consumers want. Coca-Cola's attempt to change its traditional formula was an example of a company's failure to appreciate the loyalty of Coke aficionados.

CASE IN POINT: COCA-COLA

Fisher (1985) tries to explain what happened to Coca-Cola when it attempted to change its formula to New Coke. Brand name loyalty took Coca-Cola by surprise. She reports that Coke's Chief Operating Officer Donald R. Keough says "All of the time and money and skill poured into consumer research on the new Coca-Cola could not measure or reveal the deep and abiding emotional attachment to original Coca-Cola" (p. 44). "People resented, more than anybody would have believed, that their friend was being taken away, and their friend was Coca-Cola," said John Reid, a senior vice-president of marketing for the Atlanta-based soft drink giant (Kilpatrick, 1986, p. A9).

In summary, a holistic approach is required to plan the strategy for revitalizing the organization. An organization, its workforce, and its strategies are a multi-dimensional creation. It is a system with diverse interrelating elements that all contribute to the whole organization, including human relationships, technology, and environmental responsiveness.

STAGE 3—IMPLEMENTATION OF NEW STRATEGY

The implementation stage is where all the efforts come together to produce significant changes. Central to Stage 3 is a mix of the organizational and technological domains.

Organizational Domain. Implementation has to be more than a decision to implement. Unless action follows decision, the message is to continue to do things as usual. This is why close monitoring is critical to make sure that the nonproductive routines of the past are changed. Immediate feedback is essential for making necessary changes and reinforcing new procedures.

Implementation innovations can occur not only in technology but also in resource utilization, personnel management, and productivity. Students of organizations differ on the best way to implement innovations. In regard to resource utilization, Gluck (1985) discusses the Big Bang theory. When major shifts occur in the environment, Gluck recommends tampering with the "main spring," which is similar to advocating double loop learning, as compared to single loop learning. But he warns that big bang innovation must be accompanied by the institutional courage to carry it through. Incremental innovations result from small improvements, while big bang innovation is the business equivalent of political revolution. Change has to be recognized as an opportunity for success among the trend setters of the organization or there will never be the support necessary to pull off such a climacteric.

On the other hand, Drucker (1985) takes a more conservative view. He believes that successful innovations do not occur in a blinding flash of insight, but through the careful implementation of an unspectacular but systematic management discipline. He acknowledges that introducing changes produces turbulence as well as resistance. Changing a manager's outlook from discouragement to optimism is a critical factor in opening up opportunities for creating greater efficiency. A third view is that because innovation and its implementation have tumultuous realities, they are best managed as incremental, goal oriented, interactive learning processes (Quinn, 1985).

Implementing the revitalization strategy requires harnessing what is healthy and productive and reinforcing. This means placing people where they can build on their strengths, and do what they do best. Brown (1984) faults firms which assign managers to various tasks not because they are good at the task, but because they have more seniority, or more experience. He says that

> A typical example is the assignment of a new venture responsibility to the most experienced executive, regardless of whether that manager has relevant experience, or even any entrepreneurial spirit. The evidence is mounting that assigning managers to strategies for which they are suited by experience, skill or temperament can make an important difference in organization performance. (p. 47)

Innovations in human resource management also show a variety of concerns and approaches. Strategies based on control are very different from strategies based on commitment. Eliciting worker commitment and providing the environment in which it can flourish pays tangible dividends for the individuals and for the company. One approach is a commitment among personnel to perform several tasks. In its short-lived heyday People Express Airlines limited its management hierarchy to three levels and organized its workforce into three- or four-person groups, with each position having exceptionally broad scope. Flight managers were pilots who also performed dispatching and safety checks. Customer service managers performed ticketing, security clearance, passenger boarding, and in-flight service. Everyone was expected to rotate to boost everyone's understanding of the business and to promote personal development as well as commitment (Walton, 1985).

Kanter (1983) talks about how critical people are to an organization, but how recognition of this only comes when the organization is in jeopardy. "In every sector, old and new, I hear a renewed recognition of the importance of people, and of the talents and contributions of individuals, to a company's success. People seem to matter in direct proportion to an awareness of corporate crisis" (p. 17).

A pygmalion effect works in organizations just as it does in the classroom. Supervisors who hold high expectations of subordinates' abilities may enhance those subordinates' productivity, just as in the case of the grammar school teacher who expects higher performance from her students, and usually gets it. Much of the success of the Springfield Remanufacturing Center Corporation results from expecting the most out of employees.

CASE IN POINT: SPRINGFIELD REMANUFACTURING CENTER CORPORATION

In 1983 International Harvester wanted to divest itself of an unprofitable unit called the Springfield Remanufacturing Center Corporation. John P. Stack, along with twelve other employees bought the business from Harvester and started the climb to success. SRC's sales have grown 40 percent per year through 1986 and the value of a share in the employee stock ownership plan has increased from ten cents to $8.45. Absenteeism and employee turnover have virtually disappeared and the number of accidents in the plant has dropped. Stack says this turnaround owes much to SRC's exacting quantitative controls but even more to its almost evangelical insistence on giving human potential its due. "Look, we're appealing to the highest level of thinking we can in every employee in our company. Why hire a guy and only use his brain to grind crankshafts?" (Rhodes with Amend, 1986).

In summary, communication is as critical in the implementation stage as it is in the strategy formulation stage. Employees need to be able to access reliable information whenever they need it. Likewise, they need to feel free to send information whenever they choose. Although people would like to receive information directly from superiors, most report they actually receive the majority of work related information from the grapevine. Given that the grapevine will always exist in organizations, it is essential that the formal lines of communication be open enough that rumors traveling on the grapevine can be verified through formal channels (Levson & Guy, 1987).

Technological Domain. Innovations in productivity are based not only on technological improvements but also on quality of work life programs. These are designed to decrease absenteeism and increase morale. Vandervelde (1981) says that companies need to maximize their return on people investment (ROPI). Managers must hone those soft skills many have been taught to ignore in lieu of concentrating on numbers.

Productivity innovations receive more attention than innovations in other areas because they often rely on flashy technology. One of the advantages to incorporating new technology is that it typically provides rapid feedback on its success or failure. Main (1984), for example, contrasts the introduction of quality circles to the introduction of new machinery. Quality circles implementation requires a lot more time and preparation than the introduction of machinery, and workers must be receptive to the quality circles. The American "quick fix" mentality does not lend itself to the slow process of changing people's approaches to work by implementing quality circles or other participative approaches.

Even with these drawbacks, quality circles have been used successfully to increase productivity (Werther, 1982). They call for careful planning, slow and deliberate implementation, and a genuine concern for employees' ideas. Caterpillar Tractor Company attributed a 300 percent rate of return over several years to quality circles. Werther found the following organizations to have successfully adopted some version of quality circles: IBM, General Motors, Texas Instruments, Lockheed, RCA, Westinghouse, General Electric, Control Data Corporation, Union Carbide, Tektronics, Northrop Aircraft, American Express, and Intel.

Sociotechnical Systems (STS) are a method for incorporating three sets of variables into the design of work stations and office procedures: environmental, organizational, and individual (Taylor & Asadorian, 1985). STS incorporates human preferences into the design of organizational systems along with industrial engineering. It has paid off at Volvo and GM, as well as Weyerhauser, Shell, Best Foods, and Sherwin-Williams.

STAGE 4—CEMENTING NEW ROUTINES

Freezing new procedures into place is the final step in the resurrection of the organization. Technological and organizational innovations that proved successful in Stage 3 become incorporated into organizational routines. All domains are important to Stage 4 because this is where new strategies incorporating human, organizational, and environmental domains become the accepted routine.

Keeping an institution successful is more difficult than making it successful. Chrysler Corporation is an example of a resurrection. Now that it is plateauing, the unions are demanding higher wages, Lee Iacocca is being rewarded with a $5 million bonus, and complacency is likely to set in. During 1984 it built 19.9 vehicles per employee versus 10.2 in 1980 (Flax, 1985). Computer aided design contributed to this increase in productivity. But freezing positive forces into the mindset of the work force is more than their getting used to new machinery. The communication channels that work, stay open, and provide free and easy access up and down the chain of command must be identified and maintained. Hardening of the arteries is a threat not only to human health but to the health of communication flows in organizations. When lines of communication become rigid and inflexible, they lose their usefulness and reliability as information channels.

Foresight into future pitfalls is important. Even successful Lee Iacocca admits that Chrysler, although currently resurrected, will be faced with more hurdles in a few years. In September, 1985, after recording a $2.4 billion profit after taxes, and expecting another good year (translated as clearing at least $2 billion after taxes) Iacocca is quoted as saying "We'll have a couple of good years and then get ready for the storm. I hope we don't have to give a lot back" (Mateja, 1985, p. 8B).

Human Domain. The organization must reinforce that which is desirable and reward programs and incentives that work. When personnel see employees reinforced who are contributing to the revitalization, the message is loud and clear: behave as they do. Positive values, expressions, litanies, customs, and habits must be sustained as a part of the culture. Deal and Kennedy (1982) describe various kinds of corporate cultures and show how they contribute to developing and reinforcing certain work habits. In order to socialize employees to the new culture, a symbolic manager is needed. This is the "coach" who promotes the values necessary to strengthen the culture. When an organization is attempting to change, the force of the old culture can neutralize a proposed change. What must be watched for in renewal is the natural inclination to step backward and rely on yesterday's habits and routines. The coach as manager of the new symbols plays an important role, making sure that old litanies are replaced by the new.

Organizational Domain. While corporate culture is the system of shared values and beliefs among the workforce, it interacts with personnel, structure, and control mechanisms to produce performance norms. Successful organizations possess distinctive cultures that enable them to move quickly and respond to change (Gardner, 1985). Fundamental to this facet of the organizational domain is a set of policies, procedures, and lines of authority that institutionalize some routines, yet allow as much flexibility as possible. Freezing new routines into place is a process that takes time and is not accomplished until new behaviors become old habits and actual practice reflects formal policies.

Environmental Domain. It is not enough to capture the best internal communication channels and the best of the culture within the organization, although both are essential. Communication channels with the external environment must be nurtured, along with positive perceptions of the public toward the organization.

The fourth stage requires commitment and involvement at all levels of the organization. Top management needs to augment employee participation by keeping personnel abreast of current financial results of their work, market trends, and activities of competitors. Monitoring has to be constant to make sure that counterproductive values or attitudes or habits do not also get frozen into place. Once routines are institutionalized, it is time for those at the apex of the organization to analyze the results of the strategies in place and then commit themselves to whatever changes are needed. If needed changes are not identified early enough and the organization stumbles, then the process of climbing the stairs starts again.

Technological Domain. In this cementing stage, technology's role is to facilitate routines. People should become not only accustomed to it but comfortable with it. The implementation in the third stage is proven successful in the fourth stage when employees make it clear that they have adapted their work to the technology and rely on it rather than resent it. Technology is only useful when it is fully accepted by employees and fits within the work scheme.

SUMMARY

The resurrection process can be broken into four phases, with the first laying the groundwork for the second, the second laying the foundation for the third, and finally the third laying the basis for the fourth and final stage. Skillful management and the organization's commitment are required to successfully pass from one stage to the next.

The process of revitalization involves a number of considerations. Magic potions will not do the work that must be done. A proactive management stance is essential. All facets of the organization have to be dealt with, reexamined, changed where needed, and/or held constant where needed. The best people to do the job must be selected. The best communication channels, internal and external, must be available. Constructive values in the culture must be reinforced, while values that are counterproductive are eliminated.

• The first stage is the decision and commitment phase in which top management actively decides to resurrect the organization.

• The second phase is the development of the strategies to accomplish the revitalization and securing commitment from the trend setters throughout the organization.

• The third phase is the implementation of the strategy, then identifying and rectifying the problems and unintended consequences that arise.

• The fourth stage represents the acculturation of new methods, so that they become a part of the organizational routines.

• The final stage extends into a maintenance phase. To maintain the turnaround, close monitoring of the revitalization effort is necessary, along with keeping abreast of changes in the market in order to prevent a downturn. If a downturn does occur, then the process starts over, with those at the top of the organization beginning at the first stage.

7

In the Midst of the Phoenix Syndrome: NASA and the Space Shuttle Program

The Phoenix Syndrome occurs when an organization, or unit within an organization, declines almost to the point of death and then rises out of its own ashes to flourish again. This chapter applies the stages of the Phoenix Syndrome to the Manned Space Flight Program within the National Aeronautics and Space Administration. This case study demonstrates how the phases of decline-followed-by-renewal characterize the path of NASA's manned space flight program over its thirty-year history.

As any organization ages it develops the slack resources to tolerate the effects of decline over a longer period of time. Early in an organization's life decline comes in a precipitous fashion, threatening its very survival. After an organization has matured and developed familiar routines, decline is more gradual and its effects can be tolerated longer. For exmple, in NASA's first manned space flight endeavor, Project Mercury, officials were extremely cautious before launching a man into space. They wanted to avoid a mid-flight tragedy that could jeopardize the fledgling space program. The public was impatient with how long it took to achieve the first manned launch. All was forgiven though, when an unprecedented series of safe missions followed the first manned launch in 1961. By the time a launching pad fire resulted in the deaths of three astronauts in 1967, the public was so confident of NASA's abilities that little thought was given to abandoning manned space flight. The fire delayed the Apollo program by eighteen months but did not alter the goal of landing a man on the moon. However, nineteen years after the launching pad fire, on January 28, 1986, a seemingly routine launch of the space shuttle Challenger resulted in its explosion seventy-three seconds into flight, killing seven crew members. The Challenger explosion brought the public's faith in the agency into question. Challenger's explosion was a crisis, not a cause of decline. But the crisis brought an inspection of the internal workings of the organization. The inspection shows an agency that has been in decline for years. The tragedy was simply the denouement of that decline.

NASA made no public announcement for five hours following the explosion. Senator Slade Gorton, then Chair of the Senate Subcommittee on Science, Transportation, and Space, said, "I would have hoped for a more open response on the part of NASA." He explained: "Circling the wagons is the natural human reaction, but it was the wrong response" (Corrigan, 1986a, p. 688). T. Keith Glennan, NASA's first administrator, was asked to comment on NASA's performance following the accident. He told a caller he was quite certain that NASA had not deviated from adherence to thoughtful, careful safety measures—those measures that had always been the agency's hallmark. But as he learned more about NASA's inner workings during the shuttle program, he revised his earlier opinion. Testimony revealed an agency that had become complacent about safety. Glennan decided his earlier assessment had been wrong. "Any organization that grows as that one did, and contracts as that one did and had the success that one did tends to go a little seedy after a while. You see it in government, in business, anywhere. People begin to think they've got the business well in hand" (Corrigan, 1986a, p. 686).

Despite NASA's demonstrated capability to design and operate some of the most advanced technologies conceived on this planet, the men and women of NASA proved themselves to be human and fallible. They misinterpreted the significance of masses of technical data, failed to grasp the implication of critical events, relied on routines that had worked in the past, and proved themselves vulnerable to the same stresses that threaten the quality of the simplest operation.

NASA has been hailed as the exemplar of organizational excellence. Except for occasional failings, such as the 1967 launching pad fire and the abortive flight of Apollo 13 in 1970, NASA has achieved heights in space exploration that were unthinkable a generation ago. On the ground, its management has been a model for others to follow. Its matrix organizational structure has been cited in numerous management texts as the ideal structure for motivating a team of highly skilled professionals (Galbraith, 1973; Koontz & O'Donnell, 1978; Mintzberg, 1979; Ouchi, 1981; Starling, 1986; among many others). Organizations staffed by professionals have adopted NASA's style of management in the hope of achieving a maximum level of creative output from their personnel.

It has become apparent that there were pockets of darkness in NASA's organizational behavior. Students of organizations are reevaluating their glowing appraisal of NASA. As a thirty-year-old agency, it is struggling through a mid-life crisis. A brief history of the manned space flight program follows to provide a background for understanding the events leading up to and following the loss of Challenger.

HISTORY OF NASA'S MANNED SPACE FLIGHT PROGRAM

From NACA to NASA

NASA did not spring full-blown into being in 1958. A former organization called the National Advisory Committee for Aeronautics evolved into NASA. The Advisory Committee had been established by Congress in 1915. Its mission was to supervise and direct the scientific study of the problems of flight, with the objective of learning practical solutions. NACA remained relatively small and inconspicuous but developed a reputation for originality and thorough research (Swenson, Grimwood, & Alexander, 1966). On October 4, 1957, the Soviets blasted Sputnik, the first artificial Earth satellite, into orbit. A month later, they launched Sputnik II with a dog aboard. The United States was embarrassed that the Soviets were capable of such feats and the U.S. was not. On April 2, 1958, President Eisenhower sent a formal message to Congress calling for the establishment of a National Aeronautics and Space Agency that would absorb NACA and assume responsibility for all civilian space activities. The Space Act was passed and signed into law on July 29, 1958 (P.L. 85-568). To head the new agency, Eisenhower chose T. Keith Glennan, President of the Case Institute of Technology, former member of the Atomic Energy Commission, and a staunch Republican. Glennan furnished administrative leadership for the new agency while the Deputy Administrator, who was the former director of NACA, functioned as NASA's scientific and technical overseer.

The agency has had six administrators, each serving at the pleasure of the President. T. Keith Glennan (1958-1961) served under the Eisenhower administration. James E. Webb (1961-1968) served under the Kennedy and Johnson administrations. Thomas O. Paine (1968-1970) was appointed at the end of Johnson's administration and continued to serve during President Nixon's first term in office. James C. Fletcher (1971-1977; 1986-present) served under Presidents Nixon and Ford and returned following the Challenger accident to serve under President Reagan. Robert A. Frosch (1977-1981) served during the Carter years. James M. Beggs (1981-1985) served under President Reagan. Although he was later to be acquitted, in December 1985 Beggs was indicted on charges of defrauding the Pentagon in his former job at General Dynamics. He was on a leave of absence when Challenger was launched and Deputy Administrator William Graham was in charge. With the indictment hanging over his head, and NASA's need for leadership following the accident, Beggs resigned. James C. Fletcher was then renamed administrator.

Early in NASA's history, Glennan invoked the following arguments to urge Congressional support for civilian space exploration. These have become the mainstay of NASA's justification for being: (1) the Soviets were already ahead of the United States in space research and accomplishments and their challenge demanded a vigorous response; (2) uncommitted nations would be positively influenced by U.S. space achievements; (3) space investment would pay for itself many times over in economic benefits that would enhance the lives of all Americans (McDougall, 1985).

During its first years NASA operated much the same as NACA. It behaved as a research and development agency and researchers treated each other in a collegial manner. Decentralized decision making with a high degree of respect for individual autonomy was the rule. Separate program centers developed as individual, highly motivated fiefdoms (Levine, 1982). Because of each center's unique history and pool of employees, each developed its own culture. Langley, Ames, Lewis, Goddard, and the Jet Propulsion Laboratory have been more research oriented and less program oriented, relying on more of a collegial management structure. Marshall, Kennedy, and Johnson have been program oriented. Headquarters has always been substantially different from the other centers by virtue of its responsibility for oversight and funding and its placement in the federal bureaucracy of Washington, D.C.

In order to become indispensable to the agency's future and avoid the possibility of being closed down for economic reasons, centers are tempted to become "little NASAs." As a major employer in its congressional district, each center has its congressional champions who resist any suggestion of cutting back or eliminating the installation. For this reason centers are friendly competitors, rather than full partners.

Four manned projects were undertaken in NASA's early years. Project Mercury (1958-1963) tested the ability of one man to function up to several hours in earth orbit. Gemini (1962-1966) assigned two-man crews in one spacecraft to perform a variety of tasks, including rendezvous and docking in earth orbit with a target vehicle and moving around outside the spacecraft. Apollo (1960-1972) sent three-man crews on progressively more ambitious missions culminating in the first manned lunar landing in July 1969. Skylab (1973-1974) provided a laboratory in space where astronauts conducted experiments.

Project Mercury (1958-1963)

Project Mercury was designed to meet two goals: to get a manned capsule into space as quickly as possible and to serve as the first in a three step process of landing an American on the moon. The desire to beat the Russians became a battle cry and the goal of a manned lunar landing became its own justification. Project Mercury failed to move as quickly as planners had anticipated. With no experience from prior launches, the launch team was cautious. It moved slowly, performing test after test before sending a human into space. The public rapidly lost faith in NASA's ability to beat the Soviets in a space race. A disappointed journalist published this report in August, 1960:

> NASA's Mercury manned-satellite program appears to be plummeting the United States toward a new humiliating disaster in the East-West space race. . . . The program today is more than one year behind its original schedule and is expected to slip to two. Therefore, it no longer offers any realistic hope of beating Russia in launching the first man into orbit around the earth—much less serve as an early stepping stone for reaching the moon. . . . (Swenson et al., 1966, p. 283)

As with all manned space flight projects that have followed, NASA engineers were under pressure to launch as quickly as possible. They resisted the pressure by insisting on the importance of astronaut safety and by not being willing to risk failure.

The first manned orbital Mercury mission came twenty-two months later than scheduled and three weeks after Yuri Gagarin's orbital flight. In spite of its late beginnings, Mercury achieved three successful manned launches, each of increasing technological sophistication. Alan Shepard made a suborbital flight on May 5, 1961; John Glenn orbited the earth three times on February 20, 1962; and Gordon Cooper completed twenty-two orbits on May 15-16, 1963. The Mercury flights convinced NASA and the public that humans could function normally during space flight.

As an organization NASA went through a rapid-fire succession of growing pains. Throughout its history, NASA has struggled with maintaining a decentralized agency while ensuring accountability and coordination between centers. In 1961, major structural changes were made to deal with communication and control problems throughout the agency. The revised structure only fanned flames of discord. The changes created a free-for-all between program offices at headquarters and the outlying centers (Levine, 1982).

As with any young organization the cycles of decline and renewal are compressed with little room for error. By mid-October, 1962, serious problems were confronting agency management. There were internal communication problems cutting across all organizational levels. They affected relations among headquarters and the centers, the program and functional offices, and the centers themselves. Five centers were designing and fabricating spacecraft with almost no exchange of information between them. "Headquarters was too eager to involve itself in relations with contractors, too slow to approve projects submitted by the centers, and too reluctant to encourage intercenter coordination" (Levine, 1982, p. 41). A reorganization in 1963 brought a return to the NACA concept of giving the field installations responsibility for technical decision making. The Gemini years did not see the massive reorganizations that Mercury had wrought. The 1963 reorganization had produced a decentralized management structure that department heads as well as center directors could work within (Levine, 1982). As the years passed and NASA developed comfortable routines, major changes occurred only after progressively longer intervals.

Project Gemini (1962-1966)

Project Gemini served as a precursor to Apollo's manned lunar landing. The agency geared up to do what had never been done before. Ten manned Gemini flights spanned 603 days, averaging a flight every 60 days (Hacker & Grimwood, 1977). Gemini developed the confidence of NASA officials that a scheduled series of manned launches could be accomplished safely. It proved that astronauts could leave the shelter of their vehicle and function in space, they could rendezvous with a target in orbit, and they could survive up to two weeks in orbit without ill effects. It was during the Gemini years that Mission Control Center in Houston, Texas, became operational. Houston assumed flight control duties from the former control center at what was then called Cape Kennedy.

Project Apollo (1960-1972)

President Kennedy was convinced that a manned lunar landing was the logical, inevitable way for the United States to demonstrate its superiority in space. Project Apollo's goal was to achieve his dream. In Projects Mercury and Gemini, there had been only one lead center, regardless of how many installations actually participated. Apollo was a much more complex project that could not be assigned to only one lead center. For the Apollo Project, major elements were assigned to lead centers in a manner similar to that used later with the space shuttle. The spacecraft was assigned to Houston, the propulsion system to Marshall, the tracking system to Goddard, and Kennedy was the launch site.

While the Mercury years saw growing pains in the form of accountability and communication, the Apollo years brought budgetary cutbacks and quality control problems. In 1967 the Vietnam War, combined with racial and urban unrest, resulted in the first reduction in space spending after eight years of rapid growth. As the agency faced reductions in its budget, the planned Voyager exploration of Mars was cancelled, a Civil Service Commission report was highly critical of NASA personnel management, and a General Accounting Office investigation of NASA support service contracts occurred. Furthermore, careless workmanship resulted in the first deaths of American astronauts.

On January 27, 1967, Virgil I. "Gus" Grissom, Edward H. White, and Roger B. Chaffee were killed in a launching pad fire as they sat in a practice session aboard a spacecraft that was to be the first manned launch of the Apollo program. Shortly after the accident, contractors and employees were instructed not to release any information about the fire. A notice said ". . . all NASA and contractor employees are directed to refrain from discussing technical aspects of the accident outside of assigned working situations. This is meant to rule out accident discussion with other employees, family, friends, neighbors and the like. All press information will be channeled through the Public Affairs Office" (Ertel & Newkirk with Brooks, 1978, p. 68). NASA used a similar gag order nineteen years later following the loss of Challenger.

Following the fire, questions were raised about the future of the Apollo program. In a recap of the tragedy, *Newsweek* emphasized how Projects Mercury and Gemini had rolled up a total of nearly 18 million miles in orbit and astronauts had suffered nothing physically more serious than bruised elbows and eye irritations en route. The nation was forgiving, confident, and optimistic. The press issued upbeat reports of NASA's accomplishments:

Space flight had become statistically the safest form of transportation known to man. The reasons for this superb safety record were not hard to find: long and rigorous pilot training, cautious step-by-step programs, quality control, back-up systems . . . and enormous expenditures of time and money and ingenuity to insure that every margin of safety possible had been built in." (*Newsweek*, 1967b, pp. 25-26)

After eulogizing the three dead astronauts, the article closed with:

There may well be more setbacks, more deaths. Will the U.S., then, choose to turn back from its drive to reach the moon? It doesn't seem likely. Command pilot Grissom himself once argued the case for going ahead. "If we die," he said, "we want people to accept it. The conquest of space is worth the risk of life." (p. 29)

But beyond the eulogy another side of the story crept out. Within a few weeks *Newsweek* reported that the astronauts had not died instantly, as NASA had insisted, and that the cause of the fire was due to an incredible series of miscalculations. NASA's Manned Spaceflight Director Dr.

George E. Mueller had testified before a Senate Aeronautical and Space Sciences Committee. He said NASA had permitted the spacecraft to be filled with all kinds of combustible materials and outfitted with an emergency exit arrangement "that wouldn't have been tolerated by a backwoods fire department inspector" (*Newsweek*, 1967a, p. 94). A NASA Board of Inquiry investigation revealed deficiencies in design, engineering, and manufacture, along with poor quality control (*Aviation Week & Space Technology*, 1967). Specific fingers of blame were pointed at quality control at NASA and at North American, the prime contractor for the Apollo spacecraft. There had been a number of items on board the spacecraft not documented by quality inspection records. There were inadequate reviews of possible ignition sources prior to manned tests. There was no accountability for communications problems. Test specifications for the spacecraft were unclear, incomplete, and not readily available to those who needed them. Electrical wiring was poorly designed and presented a risk that could have been prevented. Rescue personnel were not equipped to respond to a fire in the spacecraft (Normyle, 1967a).

Subsequent investigations by the House and Senate space committees uncovered other problems. First, the Apollo program manager had visited the North American Aviation plant late in 1965 and had discovered evidence of schedule slippage, bad workmanship, and a lack of direction from the senior management of North American. Second, North American had been awarded the command service module contract despite an internal NASA report that rated another company higher on technical performance. At a cost of an extra $410 million, a reorganization of North American's Space Division, and a slip of eighteen months in the launch schedule, NASA redesigned the Apollo spacecraft, removed combustible materials and drew tighter reins on its contractors (Levine, 1982). There were charges that NASA had gone too far in contracting out to the point where its essential in-house management capability was undermined (Kloman, 1985). Similar sets of problems and concerns were to be repeated nineteen years later.

Although quality control problems had been occurring for some time, it was not until they became public that the agency attended to them. In 1967, Administrator Webb created an Office of Organization and Management and gave it police authority over the system. In creating the new office, Webb was reacting to the conclusion that many NASA employees had not minded how the job was done, as long as it was done. The new office was responsible for seeing that prescribed systems and procedures were followed. It was to serve as a check on the presumed freedom of the program offices to do as they pleased and to diminish the friction between headquarters and project centers (Normyle, 1967b). NASA's 1967 uncomfortable tolerance of a public debate over its quality control mechanisms was a precursor to its 1986 behavior. Quieting critics, controlling information, and obscuring weaknesses occurred then as well as nineteen years later.

Project Apollo launched eleven flights, including six lunar landings. The first landing on the moon was achieved by Apollo 11 on July 20, 1969 and the last in December 1972. Apollo 13 had been scheduled to be the third manned lunar landing, but the landing was aborted because of the explosion of an oxygen tank in the service module en route to the moon. The flight had to return to earth as quickly as possible. A review board appointed to determine the cause of the oxygen tank failure concluded that the accident was caused by a combination of mistakes. The trouble had started when two safety switches had been accidentally welded shut by a ground test during which 65 volts of electricity—more than twice the switches' specified 28 volts—had been applied to them. Beech Aircraft Corporation, manufacturer of the oxygen tank, had failed to change the specifications for the switches five years earlier, when those for the rest of the circuit were increased from 28 volts to 65 (*Newsweek*, 1970a). Someone along the long line of checks and counterchecks had failed to see that design standards and testing standards for thermal switches were checked against each other (*Newsweek*, 1970b). Failure to detect the Apollo 13 wiring problem was an additional early warning following the launching pad fire. It warned that NASA's reliance on a contractor workforce and its ineffective quality control measures could result in tragedy. As the agency grew even more reliant on sophisticated, complex technology, it became even more vulnerable to simple mistakes made at the lowest levels.

As Project Apollo achieved its goal, public interest in space exploration waned. Landing on the moon, rather than being a means to an end of further space exploration, had become an end in itself and it had been achieved. Congress was ready to cut NASA's funds and spend the money elsewhere. *National Journal* (1970) cited an American Broadcasting Company poll indicating that 62 percent of the American people favored a cutback in NASA funds, with only 8 percent wanting an increase. In 1971 NASA was preparing to operate with its smallest budget in eight years. A vacuum developed at the center of NASA's programmatic future. The agency was confronted with an external force that contributed to decline. That force was a changing U.S. economy and a public whose opinion had changed about the worthiness of spending more funds on space exploration.

Budget cuts resulted in layoffs at the centers. These losses in manpower caused problems of their own: a rise in the average age of center personnel and an accompanying loss of new employees with their new ideas and fresh outlooks, loss of morale, and jealousy between centers. The jealousy and territoriality between centers would show up by different centers refusing to speak up for the good of the overall organization. "We found that some of the centers would not discuss the question of their staffing because they were afraid that if they indicated that they could take on a new project that they wanted to get, the availability of people would be signalled for headquarters to take those people away and put them somewhere else" (Levine, 1982, p. 263). The layoffs of junior personnel would show its effects a decade later when senior personnel approached retirement age and there would be too few well trained personnel to promote into top management positions.

Skylab (May 1973 to February 1974)

Project Apollo was followed by Skylab. It was a project serving as a trial space station, applying what had been learned during the Apollo years. An orbiting spacecraft provided life support for about nine months while astronauts conducted experiments. It was the closest NASA had ever come to having a space station. The first crew arrived on May 26, 1973 and the final crew left there February 8, 1974 (Cooper, 1976).

Space Shuttle (1969-Present)

Following the completion of the Apollo program, the manned space flight program went into a decade-long hiatus before the space shuttle became operational. NASA's history demonstrates that there is an inherent need for an on-going major project. This is not only to provide the level of funding necessary to sustain the institution but also to stimulate and inspire the work force as well as the public.

In September 1969, two months after the initial lunar landing, three possible NASA programs had been proposed by Administrator Paine. The first was an $8 to $10 billion per year program involving a manned Mars expedition, a space station in lunar orbit, and a 50-person Earth-orbiting station serviced by a space shuttle. An intermediate program costing less than $8 billion annually included the Mars mission. The cheapest proposal was a modest $4 to $5.7 billion a year program which included an Earth-orbiting space station and the space shuttle as its link to Earth. President Nixon chose the shuttle-tended space base as a long-range goal but focused on development of the shuttle vehicle as the priority. The space shuttle, earlier only the transport element of a broad, multi-objective space plan, became the focus of NASA's short-term future (Levine, 1982; Presidential Commission, 1986). This decision set the scene for another means-end inversion. Just as a lunar landing had become its own justification during the 1960s, a space shuttle became its own justification for the 1970s and 1980s.

It was in fiscal year 1971 that NASA started the design of a reusable space shuttle that would take off vertically and land horizontally, carrying people and supplies on regularly scheduled trips between earth and earth orbit. James C. Fletcher, reappointed Administrator in 1986 following the Challenger tragedy, was also the administrator then. It was Fletcher who thought the original shuttle design was too costly to win Congressional approval and advocated a cost cutting scaled-down version. His willingness to make trade-offs to accommodate a budget conscious Congress proved to be a double-edged sword. It ensured NASA's survival but resulted in less than the safest equipment. The low bid design is the one currently in use: reusable solid rocket boosters and an expendable external fuel tank (*National Journal*, 1986).

In 1977 a report was issued that recommended an organizational placement for the space shuttle program. The panel writing the report was chaired by James M. Beggs who was then executive vice-president of General Dynamics Corporation and was later to become Administrator of NASA. Several alternatives had been considered: making the space shuttle a private or government corporation; putting it within existing federal departments; creating a new independent federal agency; or leaving it within NASA itself. The panel recommended leaving it within NASA for several reasons, with the most telling argument being "To remove from NASA the most visible single space program would leave NASA with significantly less opportunity to attract funds and attention" (National Academy of Public Administration, 1977, p. 102). This repeats NASA's investment in having a single manned space flight project to attract public interest. It also foretells the commitment that NASA was about to make in operating the shuttle.

As originally proposed, the space shuttle was to last at least a hundred missions and have a two-week turnaround time. Reusability was intended to reduce the cost of putting men and payloads into orbit (Ertel et al., 1978). Although the shuttle's first flight was originally scheduled for early 1978, it did not take place until 1981 because there were persistent problems with the shuttle's propulsion system and unexpected launch stresses. Engineers discovered the orbiters could carry far less weight than originally planned and could be expected to last fifty missions rather than one hundred as originally claimed (Blakely, 1986). A longer turnaround time was required than what had been anticipated. Seven months elapsed between the first and second flights of the orbiter Columbia in 1981. By the end of 1985 the turn-around period for most flights had stabilized at around two months (Dorr, Jr., 1986).

NASA had divided managerial responsibility for the shuttle program among three of its centers: Johnson Space Center was assigned management of the orbiter; Marshall Space Flight Center was responsible for the orbiter's main engines, the external tank, and the solid rocket boosters; and Kennedy Space Center was given the job of assembling the space shuttle components, checking them out, and conducting launches. The management process NASA followed was identical to that during the Apollo program. There were structured levels of graduated decision making within the shuttle program, with Level I being the highest and Level IV being lowest. Problems were to flow from Level IV only as high as needed. If no one at a lower level could solve a problem then it was sent higher until it was solved.

NASA was well aware, even in the planning stages, that space shuttle missions would occasionally be lost. In 1979, *Aviation Week & Space Technology* reported that most malfunctions of the solid rocket boosters would not be survivable (Covault, 1979). It was also anticipated that an occasional launch abort situation would be necessary, if for no other reason than the fact that the shuttle would be flying over the course of several years and would accrue several hundred flights (Covault, 1979). The reliability of the first shuttle flights had lulled many worriers to sleep, however. Including the initial orbital tests, there were twenty-four successful space shuttle missions over a fifty-seven-month period. Columbia made seven trips, Discovery six, and Atlantis two. Challenger flew most frequently—nine times prior to its last.

During the shuttle program, productivity problems surfaced just as they had during the Apollo years. Improper workmanship was not unusual (Kolcum, 1987). Speaking in 1985 of the four years of space shuttle flights, Administrator James M. Beggs admitted:

> Over the last four years, for example, we have welded with the wrong wire; have built space structures with soft aluminum; our computers have failed due to contaminated integrated circuits; and incorrectly sized fuses have caused power loss in an important mission in space. . . . Although the world perceives NASA quality as being outstanding and NASA is consistently called upon for assistance and advice, we are not immune to the general domestic decline in productivity and quality. How could we be? We employ graduates from the same universities and high schools. (Beggs, 1985, pp. 37, 49)

As the shuttle flights became routine, NASA pressed forward with an unforgiving launch schedule. In 1986 there were fifteen shuttle missions planned (Covault, 1985). Mission 51-L, the Challenger flight, was to be one of those all important missions (Smith, 1985). Such a schedule denied the reality of how long it took to examine a returned shuttle and prepare it for a subsequent launch. For example, the shuttle flight that landed a few days before Challenger's January launch date had incurred severe brake problems. A postflight inspection revealed that there had been extensive damage to the brakes that jeopardized a safe landing for any other orbiter, since they all had similar braking systems. The extent of this damage was not known until January 30, which was two days after Challenger's flight was to have begun (*Aviation Week & Space Technology*, 1986b). Even if the Challenger launch had been successful, it may have had difficulty in landing safely. There already had been one blown tire due to brake lockup and resulting skid wear (Presidential Commission, 1986). NASA sacrificed safety to maintain an unrealistic launch schedule. The means-end inversion was taking over. Instead of using each space shuttle flight to learn more about perfecting space travel, launching missions became its own reward.

In 1983 James Beggs had made the decision to select a citizen observer-participant for shuttle flights. A clear aim of this was to do what NASA had done so well in the past—build broader public support for NASA, which would translate into higher levels of funding from Congress (Magnuson, 1986). The launch of Challenger on January 28, 1986, was to inaugurate NASA's Space Flight Participant Program. It was carrying the first private U.S. citizen into space, a public school teacher.

The Challenger Explosion and Aftermath

Shortly after the accident NASA reported that the Challenger explosion had been triggered by a rupture in the vehicle's right solid rocket motor at a point where two segments of the booster are joined during preflight assembly. Unlike the media coverage of nineteen years earlier, the media was less than gentle with NASA. *National Journal* reported:

> But after the crash, the space agency itself seemed to come unglued. Instead of teamwork, there was dissension; instead of candor, a display of cover your ass; instead of instant leadership, continuing turnover at the top. Whatever the cause of the accident might have been, another troubling question has been raised: What's happened to NASA? (Corrigan, 1986c)

Decline within the manned space flight program was uncovered in the investigation following the Challenger explosion.

Problems showed up in the way shuttle launches were managed. Insufficient consideration was being given to potentially critical engineering problems. Opportunities to make necessary changes were missed or deferred until it was too late. The agency's fans became its critics. Having acknowledged decline within the agency, they began to question whether the agency could renew itself. A senator spoke pointedly to NASA's administrator when he said: "We stand in jeopardy of entering a period where NASA is in irreversible decline" (*Aviation Week & Space Technology*, 1986d, p. 24). The question before

NASA is whether it will snap out of a telescoping downward spiral and rejuvenate itself or whether it will dwindle away and its functions be absorbed by the Department of Defense and commercial space ventures. The Challenger explosion is the turning point of the story if renewal occurs. It is the beginning of the end of the story if renewal does not occur.

THE DECLINE FOLLOWED BY RENEWAL PROCESS

The Downward Spiral

When Challenger exploded, NASA's image as an organization immune to typical bureaucratic pathologies also exploded. Studying an organization like NASA is like looking at a large room through a small keyhole. The keyhole provides a view of what is straight ahead but leaves the viewer to speculate about what lies on the periphery. For all the information that is allowed to be made public, there is much left unsaid. And to focus on one aspect of the agency is to forego focusing on other aspects. Even with this limitation, quality control is a good keyhole to look through. Used as a criterion of a well managed company, quality control provides a way of comparing an organization's public face—what it tells the public about its operations—to how it actually conducts its operations.

Common threads run throughout NASA's history: maintaining the manned space flight program as its centerpiece, successfully engineering a positive public image, using the Soviet threat as justification for additional funding, persistently struggling to centralize control in a decentralized system, having difficulty enforcing standards of workmanship within the agency and its contractor workforce, and exchanging executives between NASA's top positions and its contractors' top positions. There have not been abrupt changes or redirections in NASA's mission and goals. Such turning points often mark the course of public organizations that go into decline. But NASA has the same mission now as it had in 1958, that is to conduct civilian space exploration. NASA's justification for being is still the same as the message T. Keith Glennan sent to Congress when the agency was newborn: NASA should surpass the Soviets in space exploration, impress the world with its feats, and trust that its work will enhance the lives of all Americans.

The space shuttle program has been the center of attention for NASA's manned space flight program for over half the agency's life, and it has relied more heavily on a contractor work force and sophisticated technology than earlier manned projects had. Any organization using such highly sophisticated technology is at the mercy of basic human carelessness. Rather than being kept in the spotlight, however, quality workmanship and critical communication flows fell victim to the monotony of daily routines. They were taken for granted when they should have been constantly reexamined.

In many respects the shuttle system was not ready to meet an operational schedule, but it was functioning as if it were. Crews preparing an orbiter for launch were forced to cannibalize other orbiters for spare parts since there was an inadequate inventory of replacement parts. By so doing, employees risked misplacing wires, dropping tools, and doing other damage that would not be noticed until too late. Methods for adequately testing flight readiness were not developed until flights had been taking place for some time. In 1983 Kennedy engineers found cracks in Challenger's main engines. Shuttle managers realized after the fact that the orbiter Columbia had flown five times with engine leaks that went undetected by the test methods they were using at the time (Covault, 1983). In 1988 faulty welds were discovered in engines and solid rocket boosters when an ultrasound scanner was used. Engineers had not detected the flaws in their x-ray checks. However, after finding the problems with the ultrasound, they targeted their x-rays more precisely and found the same flaws (Sawyer, 1988).

Accomplishing the immediate requirement to prepare the next launch diverted attention from what was happening to the system as a whole. Testimony given before the Presidential Commission named to investigate the Challenger accident shows that information about problems was withheld and when gathered or provided it was ignored. The problem of leakage at the field joint of the solid rocket booster began with the second flight of the shuttle. In November 1981 inspection showed there had been in-flight erosion of the primary O-ring caused by hot motor gases. Neither NASA nor its contractors acknowledged the erosion as a problem. They treated it as an acceptable flight risk. At no time did management either recommend a redesign of the joint or call for grounding shuttle flights until the problem was solved (Presidential Commission, 1986).

There is also some indication that the Challenger explosion was not caused solely by the combination of cold temperatures and a faulty field joint. Evidence indicates that the strut between the external tank and Challenger's right solid rocket booster could have been a factor (*Aviation Week & Space Technology*, 1986a). An engineer involved with construction of the struts that attach the solid boosters to the external tank said that a reliability report issued on the struts in 1983 warned they had a design deficiency that also could have triggered a catastrophic failure (Fink, 1986).

More information on quality control issues is not hard to find. For example, in November 1985 workers had damaged a portion of a solid rocket booster that was being assembled for the Challenger launch in January. An investigation uncovered deficiencies in procedures for doing the work as well as in the quality of workmanship. Technicians responsible for assembling the stages were reported to have a lackadaisical attitude, reluctant to perform any task other than their routine one. Some had not even received the training required to be doing what they were doing. Work habits were knowingly allowed to deviate from set procedures. When problems arose, work crews were inconsistent about reporting them. Sometimes they would follow prescribed procedures for dealing with problems and sometimes they would circumvent procedures without notifying anyone (*Aviation Week & Space Technology*, 1986h).

On the morning of the Challenger launch a temperature scan at two locations on the right solid rocket booster recorded unusually low Fahrenheit temperatures of 7 degrees and 9 degrees. Those readings were far below allowable limits for flight safety. The instrument was registering correctly since it showed the left booster's surface temperature at 25 degrees, which is what was expected for the weather conditions (*Aviation Week & Space Technology*, 1986g). The temperature readings were disregarded even though NASA had wind tunnel data showing similar weather conditions could cause wind blowing across the supercold external tank to be directed onto the lower section of the right booster. This would create the potential for a refrigeration effect cold enough to freeze critical O-ring seals. Furthermore, NASA had information that O-ring seals could fail at temperatures of 50 degrees or lower (Sanger, 1986a). Launch controllers at Kennedy on the morning of January 28 simply disregarded temperature warnings.

As devastating as its results were from an engineering standpoint, the disregard for concerns about abnormally low temperatures and unacceptable launch conditions is even more important from a managerial standpoint. There was an attitude that pervaded NASA at the time of the accident. Shuttle workers were motivated to make unsound decisions because of unrelenting pressure to achieve a steady, frequent flight rate of twenty-four missions per year. Just two months after the loss of Challenger NASA was still planning on resuming flights in 1987. In fact, its plans were to make nine launches in 1987, fourteen in 1988 and eighteen in 1989 (Doherty, 1986). In a struggle to survive, the agency pursued a course that denied the reality of its decline.

NASA is an embattled agency that is being stung by competing demands for timely but safe launches. This occurs within the context of budgetary shortfalls in an agency whose work force has been gutted by layoffs for years. In defense of NASA and its woes, Donald E. Fink, says,

> we see an agency whose managers are driven to distraction by demands
> for responses to oversight from Congress and various groups and

committees; an agency whose decisions often are second-guessed by outside officials lacking the expertise to raise the right questions—much less offer answers, and an agency whose prime charter is ignored by other agency managers in their haste to fill the vacuum left by NASA inaction. (Fink, 1987, p. 11)

Decline is a prolonged suboptimization of an organization's productivity. This has been the case at NASA since the last years of the Apollo program. Both economic and subjective benchmarks are apparent. Declining resources, first in the form of budget cuts and then in the form of budget increases that only kept pace with inflation, have taken their toll on the agency. With little slack in which to operate, the failure of the shuttle program to recoup as much of its shuttle launching expenses as it had hoped has pinched the agency. Its inability to plan a realistic launch schedule has caused customers and the public to lose faith in NASA's ability to plan. This has translated into a loss of prestige. Along with the budgetary constraints and layoffs that have confronted the agency, there is a negative tinge permeating the agency just below its positive veneer. The optimism and "can do" atmosphere of the Apollo years has given way to the agency's digging in its heels and denying its problems.

NASA's service level is inadequate to meet the public's expectations and its priorities are unclear. Although shuttle flights were originally intended to recoup a substantial portion of their expenses by charging fees for commercial cargo, the return on investment has been minimal. Although the shuttle was originally designed to be an element of a space station project, it has become its own space truck operation. The agency has not had clear, direct leadership from Congress or the President, and when the indictment of Administrator Beggs was being handed down, leadership was even missing from the agency itself. Instead it has had to rely on mixed messages calling for it to retain its research and development mission while recovering expenses by carrying commercial cargo, intermittently accommodating the military's space needs, and yet remaining a civilian space program open to public scrutiny. It is to accomplish all this with safety and minimal expense.

The loss of Challenger was a benchmark, in and of itself, of decline. It was an example of service level inadequacy far more than it was an example of one orbiter being lost in an explosion. The launching pad fire in 1967 and the aborted flight of Apollo 13 functioned more as crises that served to get the agency back on track. By this time, after so many years of unclear goals, weak leadership, and personnel layoffs, what might otherwise have been just another crisis in a research and development program was far more serious. NASA officials made a poor cost-benefit choice when they decided to go ahead with the Challenger launch. They chose to launch a mission disregarding the probability of failure.

Just as with the description of Cooper Green Hospital in Chapter 1, youthful NASA went through compressed cycles of decline and renewal early in its history, but now, in the history of space travel, NASA is an old agency. It has almost two decades of benchmarks within the shuttle program alone to mark its troubled course. As a result of unpredictable annual budgets, the agency set long-range goals aside to focus its major efforts on the space shuttle. It focused on the means with little regard for the ends.

NASA's decline went undiscovered by those outside the agency and denied once discovered by those within the agency. Richard C. Cook, a former NASA budget analyst, attributes NASA officials' blindness to the agency's strong self-image that works against any impulse to admit to major problems or mistakes. Those at the upper echelons were unable to accept the serious nature of problems encountered in the shuttle program. Although warned in a 1985 memorandum by Cook that the O-ring seals left each shuttle flight vulnerable to a catastrophe, no action was taken. Three days after the Challenger explosion NASA was already starting an in-house analysis of how much it would cost to fix the O-rings. But five days after the accident Acting Administrator Graham was on national television denying any history of O-ring problems (Cook, 1986b). It was not for several weeks that O-ring failure was publicly announced as the primary cause of the accident. Maintaining a positive public image has always been important to the agency, and it has been more successful at it than has any other public agency. In fact, critics joke that while some agencies have a public affairs office, NASA is a public affairs office that has an agency (Sanger, 1986b).

When the agency needed to be using double loop learning it was using single loop learning. In other words, if and when problems were identified and acted upon, corrections were made only to the problem itself. The underlying premise was not reexamined but should have been. Not only mechanical problems but also overall goals of the space shuttle program should have been reconsidered as it became more and more apparent there were inadequate resources to emphasize safety. As development of the space station was delayed time and again, new long-range goals should have been developed.

NASA has tried to stem further budget cuts by positively influencing public opinion. Its method has been to make each shuttle flight a media event. NASA's public face has shown a progressive agency, effectively conquering the unknowns of space travel. According to its theory, if it could launch spectacular missions, it could expect to garner the Congressional support necessary to maintain funding for the year to come. Scrupulous concern for safety had to be diminished in order to launch missions in as quick succession as possible. NASA officials became accustomed to bargaining and compromising their way into continued space exploration. A goal of safe space exploration was exchanged for a compromise that included more flights and a little less safety (Mann & Carter, 1986).

The other chapters in this book describe enduring characteristics of organizations as they move into and climb out of decline. The next few pages provide examples of how these characteristics were manifested in the space shuttle program and specifically in the Challenger launch decision. The stages of decline patterned in Chapter 3 appear in NASA's manned space flight program: recognition of decline, stress on the system as a result of the recognition, restricted information flow, circling the wagons, finger pointing, collective rationalization, defective decision making, and continued decline.

Recognition

When Administrator Webb was tempted to succumb to public pressure and request engineers to speed up the process for launching a manned satellite, engineers convinced him that it would be safer to launch a chimpanzee first. Webb was feeling pushed by the fact that the Soviets had already launched two manned flights. He was taking the heat for NASA's failure to move faster. He wondered why NASA engineers insisted on flying a chimp first, since Russia had already demonstrated that a man could survive a launch unharmed. But at that time, NASA was unwilling to compromise the safety of an American astronaut. The goal of safety overrode the goal of a speedy launch. Twenty-five years later Mission 51-L had been delayed twice and engineers did not successfully prevail to delay the flight again. At the time of the launch Robert K. Lund was working as the vice-president of engineering for Morton Thiokol, the contractor that made solid rocket boosters for the shuttle. Because he was concerned about cold temperatures, he testified that in a prelaunch telephone conversation he told his superior he did not want to fly. That is not what NASA wanted to hear. He agreed to recommend a launch after being told by his superior to "take off his engineering hat and put on his management hat" (Presidential Commission, 1986, p. 94). A turnabout of reasoning occurred with no one fully aware of it. Somewhere along the line officials had exchanged the goal of safe space exploration for the goal of launching missions as quickly as possible. It was not until after Challenger was lost that this was publicly recognized.

Prior to that launch, recognition of NASA's problems was manifested in denial. Implications inherent in the trade-off between safety and rapid launches were swept under the rug. The fact that mechanical problems on a returning orbiter were not discovered until the next had already been launched was disregarded. The fact that there was an inadequate supply of replacement parts was not allowed to delay flights. Orbiters on the ground were scavenged to provide parts for the shuttle on the launching pad. As problems compounded they were buried rather than corrected. Denial built up, serious problems were not talked about, and the pressure was unrelenting.

Stress

On January 27, 1986, one day before the Challenger launch, the General Accounting Office notified NASA that a Senator had requested a GAO study of shuttle delays and cost overruns (Kloman, 1986). The costs of operating the shuttle fleet far exceeded projections while revenues from users were falling short of targets. The frustrated agency responded to these interrogations by speeding up their operations and overlooking concerns about quality.

As problems were denied and a business-as-usual facade prevailed, obvious frustrations boiled to the surface. Technicians felt the pressure as they prepared orbiters for launch. They reported that early in the shuttle program employees were not disciplined for accidental damage done to an orbiter, provided the damage was fully reported when it occurred. As they were required to process launches more and more quickly, pressure built up. The forgiveness policy was not practiced. They were punished if they admitted they had accidentally caused damage. So they dealt with this by not consistently reporting damage when it occurred (Presidential Commission, 1986). Managers unwittingly communicated the pressure they felt to overlook problems in order to maintain the launch schedule. The message filtered down to employees at the lowest level. Workers feared losing their jobs. It was safer to bury bad news and only send good news up the chain of command.

Although there are other elements with faulty designs that leave the space shuttle vulnerable, the O-rings on the booster rockets have gotten the most attention since the Challenger accident. By mid-1985 one engineer reported that, because of the faulty O-rings, he held his breath each time the shuttle went up (Cook, 1986b).

Restricted Information Flow

With unrelenting pressure to meet the demands of an accelerating flight schedule and with inadequate resources to do this well, management operated in a crisis mode. It fell back on routines it knew best, and did not seek out, or attend to, information that was contrary to its own beliefs and opinions. Inspectors gathered trend data from postflight investigations but failed to analyze it and make trends and problems visible. Staff at lower levels did not send bad news up to the next level for fear of recrimination. Even with the launch decision itself NASA chose to minimize engineers' reservations about launching in cold weather and did not pass the reservations up the chain of command.

Once Challenger exploded, NASA officials disappeared from sight and made no formal announcement until several hours after the accident. At that time they announced the impoundment of all documents and materials related to the Challenger launch. They ordered all employees associated with the manned space flight program to say nothing to anyone about the accident. They immediately restricted the flow of information so those inside ''the circle'' could control it. In the testimony that followed the accident, it became apparent that the information flow across management levels was even more restricted in practice than provided for by agency policy.

The cross-feed of significant and meaningful information among those who had a need to know did not occur. Bad news was discouraged and filtered out of the pipeline. Those in leadership positions had a vested interest in sticking their collective thumb in the dike and blocking news they did not want to acknowledge. Shortly after the Presidential Commission convened and started hearing testimony about solid rocket booster problems, it received an anonymous letter charging that officials at Marshall Space Flight Center had destroyed weekly bulletins containing reports on problems with the solid rocket boosters. When interrogated, Marshall officials admitted to destroying weekly status reports and claimed the reports were simply informal means of communication and were to be routinely destroyed (Associated Press, 1986d).

Corrigan (1986b) reports on the breakdown in the human chain of command that became apparent early in the post-Challenger investigations. Rockwell International had been concerned about ice on the launching pad. Rocco Petrone, former Apollo Program Director for NASA and now president of Rockwell's Space Transportation Systems Division, said he told company staffers ''Let's make sure that NASA understands that Rockwell feels it is not safe to launch.'' That message was modified when it was relayed to NASA, according to testimony by another Rockwell executive, to a milder statement that ''Rockwell cannot assure that it is safe to fly.'' Even the softened version was never clearly communicated to Levels II and I. Arnold D. Aldrich, manager of NASA's shuttle program, said he thought that when the warning got to him, that Rockwell had expressed only a ''minor concern'' about ice (Corrigan, 1986b, p. 674).

Circle the Wagons

Top management circled the wagons, controlling exposure of NASA's soft underbelly to the public. Of course, this had been the practice of

NASA for many years. In 1975 a NASA aerospace engineer had complained publicly that the agency was throwing money away, not doing enough in-house work, and not controlling the contractors. As a result of speaking out, he was demoted and penalized with a $10,000 salary cut (Dunnavant, 1986). The higher the stakes became, the more control was exerted. It was not until witnesses came forward in the Challenger investigations that it became obvious just how tightly circled the wagons were. Allen McDonald and another Thiokol engineer had testified before the Presidential Commission that there had been significant problems with the seals on the solid rocket boosters and that they had unsuccessfully urged a postponement of the January 28 launch. Shortly after the testimony Lawrence Mulloy, the NASA official who aggressively pushed for the launch, tried to intimidate him. McDonald realized how much Mulloy and Marshall Space Flight Center wanted to control the flow of information to the Presidential Commission when Mulloy stormed into his office and slammed the door. Mulloy demanded to know why he insisted on giving information to the commission without first going through Thiokol's management or NASA's (Cook, 1986a). Both Thiokol engineers who had testified against the launch decision were reassigned following their testimony. They interpreted the move as punishment on the part of NASA and Thiokol. The wagons were circled and those who disagreed with the ingroup were excluded from the team.

The ingroup even extended to the Presidential Commission named to investigate the accident. Even though the Commission was created to investigate NASA, over half its members had a vested interest in making NASA look as good as possible. According to the *Orlando Sentinel* its members had been handpicked by NASA Acting Administrator William Graham, and President Reagan accepted most of those nominated by Graham. Seven of its thirteen members had direct ties to NASA: an astronaut, a former astronaut, a consultant to NASA, a designer of the shuttle engine, the former director of the Pentagon's shuttle program, and an executive of one of the companies that serves as a subcontractor to NASA (Cook, 1986a). Many pointed questions that could have been asked never were. Testimony that could have been explored more fully was not.

Finger Pointing

Finger pointing is practiced in earnest when the stakes are high. Because of its decentralized structure and geographic separation of centers, the agency will always have this to some degree. But it is exaggerated in the shuttle program and especially when there was a search for "the culprit" that caused the Challenger accident and brought the agency's troubles into the limelight. The true cause of the accident was that top management permitted, if not actually encouraged, staff to overlook problems. This attitude had permeated all levels of the work force. Other NASA centers were blaming Marshall Space Flight Center and officials there were busily trying to shift responsibility to Morton Thiokol. Pinning the blame on Marshall Space Flight Center did not exculpate the rest of the agency. It served only to exaggerate the divisiveness that existed between the centers.

Happily, other centers wiped their brows while Marshall took the heat for the Challenger explosion. Had a different system failed, it is just as likely that Marshall would be wiping its brow and another center would be roasting. Each center has developed a jealous pride in its own work and has shown an unwillingness to respond constructively to criticism from those in other centers.

The habit of blaming other centers begins at the top of the agency. For example, shortly after Fletcher was reappointed administrator in 1986, he started defending headquarters. He claimed that Marshall officials had not informed headquarters staff of problems. Speaking at a Congressional hearing "Before the accident occurred, perhaps we (NASA headquarters) should have been alerted" Fletcher said referring to the O-ring problems. A Congressman responded "It's not a question of you should have been alerted. You were alerted. In 1983, information came up to NASA headquarters in Washington that things had gone awry" (Brinkley, 1986, p. A8). As Fletcher tried to lay the blame on Marshall, he was called for misrepresenting the situation. There was documentation proving that headquarters had known of problems for a long time. But Fletcher, although new to the post and brought in to turn the agency around, had quickly adopted one of the agency's bad habits.

Collective Rationalization

There was tacit agreement from top management down to the shop floor to rely on routines used in each former launch. As each flight returned safely, it was easier and easier to become complacent and rely on routines once again. Problems with O-rings, brakes, struts, and other problem elements were routinely ignored, or if noted, filed away without action. Those who dissented were threatened with exclusion from the ingroup. Since a major correction of the shuttle's design problems would have slowed the launch schedule and required spending dollars on corrections that could otherwise be used on operations, an illogic became the norm. As each successive flight returned safely, calculated risks turned into an illusion of safety. Since the space shuttle program involved what seemed to be a more routine function than the earlier manned space flight projects, NASA officials made a mistake. They failed to realize how repetition and pressure to maintain a relentless launch schedule serve as a disincentive for continuous quality control. They ignored messages to the contrary and convinced themselves of their illusions.

NASA was created to be a research and development agency that designed projects of graduated sophistication within finite time limits. The shuttle program does not fit smoothly into the fabric of an agency whose prime mission is research and development. Repetitive shuttle launches are a routine operation and NASA's culture and structure do not accommodate them well. Those at the top failed to acknowledge the shift from research and development to routinized operations. Instead, they relied on past routines rather than developing and enforcing new procedures that could accommodate both the routine function of repetitive launches and the supersophisticated technology that had to be readied for each mission. As the newness of the shuttle launches wore off, people became more relaxed in the degree of scrutiny they used before making a launch decision. Officials came to believe in NASA's image—that it would succeed at making safe launches. They were lulled into a false sense of confidence and they fought to retain the illusion when confronted with information to the contrary. Even those outside NASA fell into the collective rationalization.

Recalling a prelaunch discussion, a Thiokol engineer's testimony gives an example of this collective rationalization. He testified he did not realize the impact of the discussion until it was over:

> I guess I didn't realize until after that meeting and after several days that we had absolutely changed our position from what we had been before. But that evening I guess I had never had those kinds of things come from the people at Marshall. We had to prove to them that we weren't ready, and so we got ourselves in the thought process that we were trying to find some way to prove to them it wouldn't work, and we were unable to do that. We couldn't prove absolutely that that motor wouldn't work. (Presidential Commission, 1986, p. 94)

Trained Incompetence

In what amounts to trained incompetence, staff accommodated to the routine, unquestioning acceptance of risk. Even when staff were aware of a significant probability of error, they continued to perform their routine duties, rather than risk ostracism if they were to blow the whistle on the problems they saw. Trained incompetence manifested itself in overconformity. The solid rocket boosters, even with the erosion and blow-by, had worked on twenty-four previous launches. Complacency became the rule. NASA general manager Philip Culbertson said that twenty-four successful missions probably had led the agency to a false confidence. "Probably, we got a mental attitude that was concentrated too much on operations. We discouraged redesign; that may have contributed to the problem" (*Aviation Week & Space Technology*, 1986f, p. 17).

The unquestioning risk taking that resulted and the accommodation to it became a trained incompetence. Acting in a different environment it is quite likely that staff would have insisted on correcting the problems rather than ignoring them. Even routine prelaunch safety precautions were ignored. For example, Morton Thiokol skipped three of seven mandatory safety inspections of O-rings in the solid rocket booster whose explosion destroyed the space shuttle Challenger (Associated Press, 1986a).

Immediately following the Challenger explosion, there was a surge of attention to safety, but within a year employees were sensing what they called a business-as-usual attitude. Among managers and engineers alike there was an unhealthy level of skepticism concerning the agency's commitment to safety. A year and a half after the loss of Challenger, NASA employees were reporting the same double message they received prior to the accident. "Their words say safety, but their actions say don't worry about it" (Hotz, 1988, p. 1A).

Defective Decision Making

The goal of each shuttle launch beginning a safe civilian exploration of space gave way to the goal of getting as many launches accomplished within the shortest time frame possible. The goal of safety was displaced by the goal of showing how the shuttle could carry commercial payloads with as short a turnaround time as possible.

Conflicting goals were expected of staff, so conflicting actions resulted. Reliance on routines for the sake of achieving short turnaround times resulted in unreasoned risk taking. The system was emphasizing routines, not exceptions, on a project that was anything but routine. Like putting the fox in the hen house, safety, reliability, and quality assurance offices at Kennedy and Marshall were placed under the supervision of the very organizations and activities whose efforts they were to check.

Safe civilian space exploration is the ostensible goal of NASA. The truth is that the agency responds to multiple goals, some of which are mutually exclusive. NASA's justification for carrying commercial cargo was to recoup costs by carrying commercial payloads into space. Part of the pressure to minimize turnaround time resulted from a decision to launch as many payloads as possible. Short turnaround time demands a concentrated attention to quality control to ensure each flight's safety. But as the shuttle program was gearing up to become operational, the number of quality control personnel was reduced. Between the mid-1970s and 1986 there had been a 71 percent decrease in quality control personnel (King, 1986).

In the midst of concerns about too little money, NASA followed a procurement course that allowed outrageous expenses. The *Miami Herald* reported that NASA paid $159,000 for a $5,000 fan and $315 each for wire fasteners that were available to NASA for $.03 each. NASA allows its contractors to order equipment from subcontractors and then add their own middleman's fees to the price charged the agency. A former auditor at Kennedy Space Center said "the money wasted on loafing work crews, excessive markups on parts, and freeloading contractors rivals the worst of the military" (Sachs & Cary, 1986, p. 1). Given that NASA cut back on safety staff, slashed shuttle reliability programs, and abandoned backup safety features to save money shows that its decision making has flaws.

A problem NASA has had to tackle is how to separate the significant information needed by each level from the massive amounts of data available. The agency has always followed the principle of redundant reporting systems in the theory that important information would float to the top through one channel or another. The assumption is that those at the top would make the right decision. The decision to launch Challenger calls this assumption into question. Even when the information did flow to the appropriate decision makers, it was ignored.

Continued Decline

NASA had become a combination research and development/bus company, trying to do cutting-edge research and development while attempting to get the shuttle into operational status as a routine space transportation system. In the midst of such a contradictory effort, the agency failed to acknowledge that a revised management structure would be necessary to monitor shuttle operations.

Special effort will be needed to change the attitude of those at NASA who have accommodated to the double message to maintain a demanding launch schedule while maximizing safety. Tasks must be redefined, old problems given new attention, and minds must be newly engaged. This presents a special problem for NASA, however, as the agency's work force is dominated by an unusually high proportion at retirement age. In fact, in 1985, 67 percent of NASA's work force was eligible for retirement (Kloman, 1985). When cuts were made after the Apollo program, entry-level ranks were decimated. This starved the agency of its lifeblood—new people with new energy, imagination, and new ways of looking at things. Rules became entrenched. As management ranks grayed, all the requirements of an entrenched bureaucracy developed. A well entrenched bureaucracy is appropriate when its functions are routine and there are procedures in place for ensuring quality control and good communication between departments, but there were not. The tacit understanding was that people would behave in the highly motivated research and development manner of the past. There was a practiced oblivion to the realities of routinized shuttle launches.

The race to the moon represented a clear goal set by President Kennedy and promoted by President Johnson. Although the Apollo program had a clear-cut goal, the space shuttle has not been so blessed. No clear national priorities were spelled out. The decision to begin the shuttle was made by President Nixon shortly before the Watergate scandal broke. Its development continued during the weakened presidencies of Ford and Carter. During the Reagan years NASA watched the Department of Defense's Strategic Defense Initiative budget escalate and jealously guarded its own. In the absence of effective presidential direction, NASA turned the shuttle into an all-purpose tool for space activities and aggrandizing public support.

Because it does not provide a required service, such as national defense or social security, the agency is politically vulnerable. Although it has a strong record of public support it has a mixed history of financial support. NASA has had to deal with the uncertainty of not knowing what next year's budget will bring. Research and development is a luxury to be afforded in affluent times and cut when budgets are tight. In 1968 NASA's work force had climbed to a peak of about 35,000, many of whom were involved in managing a contractor work force of approximately 400,000. There were massive layoffs in the 1970s followed by a subsequent build up to support shuttle missions in the 1980s. By 1985 NASA employed about 21,400 full-time employees.

Between Decline and Renewal

NASA's ability to remain lean has helped it accommodate to changing space initiatives. However this prevents it from being able to pick and choose among experienced personnel when it comes time to promote from mid-level ranks. There is a scarcity of potential leaders between the ages of 30 and 40—a gap caused by low recruiting levels in the 1970s, and parochialism has occurred. Few high level staff have work experience at more than one center. In 1985, of 170 Senior Executive Service employees who were surveyed at headquarters, the survey showed only 31 had been stationed in the field since 1976. And of those 31, 15 had spent their field time at Goddard Space Flight Center in the Washington suburb of Greenbelt, Maryland (Corrigan, 1986b).

Just as it did following the Apollo fire, NASA reorganized following the Challenger explosion. It reassigned major manned space flight responsibilities to NASA headquarters. This centralized authority at headquarters and lessened the independence of NASA centers. It is assumed that the focus on centralized headquarters management will reduce the trend toward parochialism that tended to grow at the centers before the Challenger accident (*Aviation Week & Space Technology*, 1986c).

A more realistic estimate for a shuttle launch schedule has been developed. By the early 1990s, the space shuttle should be flying about a dozen missions per year, far from the twenty-four originally anticipated. Confidence has also drained away from the belief in the safety and reliability of the shuttle. A vehicle with a 97.5 percent reliability factor flying thirty-one missions can expect only 53 percent of its missions to be incident-free and a vehicle designed with 99.5 percent reliability flying eithty-three flights could be expected to perform only 66 percent of the time without malfunctions occurring (Covault, 1987).

NASA also established an Office of Safety, Reliability, and Quality Assurance at headquarters. George A. Rodney, 65, an executive at Martin Marietta Orlando Aerospace Company, was named to fill the new position of Associate Administrator for Safety, Reliability, and Quality Assurance. Responsibilities include overseeing all NASA programs, reviewing NASA safety practices and standards, directing the investigation of all NASA accidents, assuring that a trend analysis program is conducted that includes accurate reporting of problems, and assuring that safety issues are considered during all reviews of manned and unmanned operations (*Aviation Week & Space Technology*, 1986e). Safety, Reliability, and Quality Assurance personnel are to be present at all significant flight readiness events and meetings to discuss flight hardware problems. Rodney will have a vote on whether or not to launch future missions. Safety officials also are attempting to provide a channel for middle and lower level managers and workers to voice safety concerns to senior management (Foley, 1986). But one year after the new department was created, an internal report checking on the status of NASA's newfound emphasis on safety concluded that a deep seated commitment to safety was still lacking. The report also concluded that there are too few safety personnel with adequate training to perform in-depth safety checks. Although space systems engineering skills are necessary to independently analyze potential risks, too many safety personnel do not have the training. As late as 1987, risk assessments were still found to be incomplete and superficial (Hotz, 1988).

The aftermath of the Challenger explosion requires a mid-course correction within NASA far more pervasive than that which followed the 1967 Apollo launching pad fire. Brought back to guide NASA during this time was 66-year-old James C. Fletcher, the former NASA administrator who thought the original shuttle design too costly to win Congressional approval and selected a scaled-down version (*National Journal*, 1986). Shortly after Fletcher's appointment, 64-year-old Dale D.

Myers was named deputy administrator. Myers was NASA associate administrator for manned space flight during Fletcher's first term as NASA administrator. Myers also had served as Rockwell International vice-president and space shuttle program manager from 1969 to 1970, and North American–Rockwell vice-president and program manager for the Apollo Command/Service Module program from 1964 to 1969. NASA's new top management are the same people who chose the original shuttle design. They also have had cozy relationships with NASA contractors over the years. Whether they can break themselves and the agency out of the business-as-usual pattern remains to be seen.

The agency is restructuring consistent with the Presidential Commission's recommendations. Matrix is out. A clearer chain of command is in. Just as other organizations are learning, a matrix structure does not ensure accountability. Only a pervasive reliance on individual responsibility does. A layer of safety personnel superimposed over NASA's work force will not change the quality of work. At best it will send a message that safety is important, and it will intercept occasional samples of flawed workmanship. True improvement must come from workers who believe that their work is critical to each mission and they must perform each task carefully and correctly. They must see themselves as the critical element of each mission. It will be management's responsibility to convince themselves of this fact and then convince everyone else in the work force of it.

Although chance inevitably played a hand in the Challenger accident, change is the more significant influence. Changes had occurred in NASA's level of resources, the clarity with which its goals were framed, and the care with which its work force performed daily tasks. The agency, as well as the people within it, were clinging to yesterday's solutions and procedures, oblivious of the need to reexamine its basic operations. They patched when they should have reevaluated the entire picture. NASA is currently between decline and renewal. It has made changes since Challenger but it has to demonstrate a renewed, sustained vigor.

Perhaps the story of Challenger is that too much of a bad thing can be good. Perhaps NASA will grab ahold of its bootstraps and pull itself up to be as good as it can be. The exciting and tough phase of its growth as an agency is now—while it teeters between losing its accomplishments to a museum shelf or becoming even more dynamic than it was in the Apollo years.

Resurrection Process

Some critics believe that never again should one project dominate NASA at the expense of other programs the way the space shuttle has. But the agency has always been motivated by one central manned space flight project. To shift the focus to unmanned projects is certainly possible and reasonable. It would involve a significant redirection of the agency, however. Whatever direction the agency travels, there are several things it is going to have to do well. It is going to have to be responsive to plural environments, meeting the public's expectations of spectacular launches, meeting the scrutiny of the General Accounting Office audits, and meeting demands of its self-imposed launch timetable. It must replace the "ho-hum" attitude toward safety with a metanorm of scrupulously careful work. The metanorm must pervade all levels of the agency and generate norms promoting careful attention to detail and an openness to examining problems and correcting them.

Within itself NASA has forces for renewal that can be harnessed. The underlying force is the work force's pride and identity with the nation's most popular public agency. There are movers and shakers at all levels who influence those around them. Their enthusiasm must be reinforced because harnessing their energy and influence paves the way for pulling the agency forward and upward rather than backward. And it capitalizes on strengths at all levels, from the shop floor to the administrator's office. NASA can make heroes of those engineers who voiced concerns about O-rings and other problem elements by now applauding their unheeded warnings. Such action is an excellent way to send an unambiguous message that a turnaround has occurred. It is more efficient to strengthen potential leaders within the organization than to impose leadership from outside the agency. Strong leadership can be exerted to channel the agency in the path it must follow. Not only unambiguous and meaningful, but also realistic, goals must be developed and communicated. Communication lines must be kept open, "can-do" cultural norms reinforced, and technology kept up-to-date and adaptable.

In order to resurrect itself, the agency will go through the following stages of renewal: decision and commitment from the top, strategy and consensus, implementation of the new strategy, and cementing new routines. Within the resurrection process all four domains will have to be targeted: the human factors of motivation, timing, and style; the organizational domain including the chain of command and goal clarity; the environmental, dealing with political forces and getting the public behind its efforts; and technological, with keeping machines and information systems in top running order.

Decision and Commitment from the Top

Strong leadership for an agency such as NASA means leadership not only within the agency but also in the White House. It was Lyndon Johnson, first as Vice-President and then as President, who played a key role in engineering the Apollo project. Presidential leadership has been missing during the shuttle program. An example of the nation's response to the Challenger accident is mirrored by S. Fred Singer, who wrote an essay for *Newsweek* urging that the U.S. space effort pursue a trip to Mars. "The Challenger disaster has shaken our faith in NASA and dramatic action is required now to keep the promise of space exploration alive. We need to establish a specific goal that can fire our imagination with demonstrable scientific and economic results. . . ." In summary to his argument he cites the Challenger explosion and says: "By announcing our intention to send Americans to Mars, we could transform a humiliating setback into a collaborative effort . . . " (Singer, 1986, p. 13). Singer is not alone in editorializing for a Project Mars. A Space Goals Task Force of the NASA Advisory Council also recommended a manned Mars goal. Specifically, it called for an unmanned exploration of Mars first, followed by increased research to build the technological base that would be needed to support development of a manned Mars expedition. The task force believed a Mars objective, which has been put on hold since the late 1960's, would enhance NASA's standing with the public and stimulate more interest in space research (*Aviation Week & Space Technology*, 1987c). President Reagan officially endorsed a manned Mars expedition when he signed the 1988 National Space Policy. This may be just what the agency needs to help it get on track again. This policy will set NASA on a course for an eventual manned lunar base in preparation for a manned flight to Mars. The two key goals of the policy are maintaining U.S. preeminence in manned Earth orbital flight and extending U.S. manned operations beyond Earth into the solar system. NASA has created a new Office of Exploration to handle the planning phases of the project. The lunar base is planned to be installed about the year 2000. It would involve three manned landings on the moon in a vehicle carrying four astronauts. Options for operations at a base on Mars through the year 2035 are being developed (Covault, 1988). This policy reaffirms what NASA does best: coordinating the creative works of scientists and engineers as they plan and put together projects to explore unexplored territories. This may energize the agency and the public more so than a space station in earth orbit.

Strategy and Consensus

There is a significant challenge before NASA as it pursues its short-range plans for a space station and while it develops long-range plans for a Mars expedition. The challenge has more to do with style than substance. It has to do with whether getting the space station operational and planning the Mars expedition will supersede NASA's attention to ensuring quality control measures. If the agency lets itself be swept off its feet by cries for speedy launches and speedy programs, history is bound to repeat itself regardless of the project at hand. Leadership outside the agency as well as inside, from the lowest levels of management to the highest, must explicitly agree on scrupulous attention to quality control and must transmit this message throughout the agency and to its contractors. Old habits die hard and it is up to NASA to make sure its bad habits die. Will it be the Space Station Project or the Mars expedition that will bring the manned space flight program back into focus, or will quality control be what brings the program back into focus? Or will it be both? For NASA to repeat its past glory, it will have to be both. It must focus on a project with unambiguous goals and apply stringent quality control to all work. Neither a focus on quality nor a focus on project will be successful for very long. A focus on quality without launching spectacular missions will cause the agency to fade from the public eye. A focus on project without adequate quality control will cause another tragedy with lives lost. The public may not forgive the agency if another accident follows too closely on Challenger's heels.

Implementation of New Strategy

Once NASA commits itself to creating renewed vigor it must implement the decision. Not unlike other organizations with a highly sophisticated work force, NASA must revise its customary way of operating and pay attention to those at the bottom. Simply rearranging personnel at the top ranks will have little if any impact on the quality of work on the shop floor. An even greater emphasis on individual responsibility for communication and vigilance will be required. As an organization, NASA has a culture that must be changed before it can soar again. In a discussion of innovative organizations, Peter Drucker says that demanding great self-discipline of personnel goes beyond the matrix structure and reflects the organization of tomorrow (Drucker, 1988). This is the challenge before NASA—to create an organization for tomorrow with today's work force.

Cement New Routines

NASA's next project is the permanently manned space station. In December 1987 NASA issued $5 billion in contracts to aerospace companies to start work on a manned space station. NASA was working on the assumption that it would receive $767 million in Fiscal 1988 for the space station. By January 1988 Congress directed NASA to reconsider its plans for the space station and develop a scaled down version budgeted at only $425 million in Fiscal 1988 (Foley, 1988). Each time NASA attempts to cut costs to make the station politically feasible it has to trade off cost for program risk. This is the same set of compromises that resulted in the shuttle design. In all likelihood the space station project will repeat the erratic budget patterns that caused fifty formal budget revisions to occur in the space shuttle program. Senator Jake Garn, one of NASA's ardent supporters, and one who was given a complimentary flight on a shuttle mission to reward his support, complained in late 1987 that there was not enough support for space in Congress or among the public (*Aviation Week & Space Technology*, 1987a).

Handling budget frustrations will be a challenge to NASA's leadership that it did not master in the past with its unrealistically low cost estimates and unrealistically high promise of number of missions to be launched. But there is a glimmer of hope that the lesson has been learned. Andrew J. Stofan, NASA associate administrator for the space station, complained about Congress' lack of support of the space station. He said there are lots of alternatives to meet cost cutting and one of them is to shelve the space station all together. He followed that comment up with the statement that "Carrying out space initiatives quickly and aggressively is possible only with strong leadership in the White House, Congress and NASA" (*Aviation Week & Space Technology*, 1987b, p. 19).

Change must penetrate the organization from the top level to the very bottom level. Whether this has happened and will be maintained is the question as the nation watches NASA prepare for more shuttle flights, develop its manned space station, and plan for a Mars mission. Whether it has done enough to revitalize itself is the question being asked. Looking through the keyhole only provides a look at a segment of the organization, but rejuvenation has to occur in all segments. Clearly, adding a layer of safety personnel will not be adequate if the leadership is not committed to a focused attention on safety. NASA has yet to convince everyone that the message is so clear that their employees and their contractors understand the demand to produce defect-free materials.

The new space policy may be the key not only to renewing the agency but to rejuvenating it. This is where the story ends, with the nation watching and hoping. Truly as a phoenix rises from the ashes, NASA can soar again if it corrects the bad habits it developed over the past years. Because it is a public agency and because the nation is watching, NASA will be operating in a fishbowl, open to public scrutiny. The stakes are high for the agency and everyone will be watching.

8

Beyond the Decline-Followed-by-Renewal Process

THE PHOENIX SYNDROME AS METAPHOR

As a metaphor, the Phoenix Syndrome traces the path of an organization's decline almost to its dissolution. At a critical point just before its death, it is transformed. The organization renews itself, rising from its own ashes to thrive again. This process is not an unusual one. Numerous examples have been provided in the chapters of this book. The process starts when an organization spirals downward and the decline is not stopped until the organization is on the verge of self-destruction. Rather than meet its demise, however, it resurrects itself to flourish once again. When the Phoenix Syndrome happens in reality, it is a compliment to the vitality of an organization and the people who staff it. To pull out of decline and return an organization to the point at which it flourishes once again is a true test of leadership and managerial skills.

An important message of the decline-followed-by-renewal process is that too much of a bad thing can be good. In other words, too much decline may be the impetus needed for managers to recognize what is happening to their organization. Although stopping the downward spiral becomes more challenging the deeper into it the organization is, a turnaround is possible, and the organization can flourish again. Chrysler is an example. Disney is an example. Both these organizations dwindled until their health became so frail that stakeholders agreed something had to be done. With Chrysler the turnaround came with an infusion of government-backed loans and strong, clear leadership. Plants were modernized, inventory procedures were streamlined, and wage concessions were achieved. At Disney the turnaround came sooner. It came after business at its theme parks had stabilized to such a point that continual growth had stopped and the decision had to be made whether to diversify or be satisfied with an aging, stagnant company. The turnaround effort brought a renewed vigor to the corporation and a successful diversification into movie production. In both these cases, the critical mass necessary to stop the decline and turn it around was not present until the situation had progressed to the point it was noticeable to many people. This is the second message of the decline-followed-by-renewal process. Decline will be stopped not when it is first noticed by someone, but when it is noticed by enough people to create the enthusiasm and commitment to initiate a renewal strategy.

There are enduring characteristics that accompany decline, whether the organization is a business or a public or nonprofit agency. In the downward spiral these characteristics begin with recognition that a problem exists. There is a reaction to this acknowledgment. Those aware of the problem sequester themselves away from outsiders either to contain the information or choose a course of action. The information flow becomes restricted and boundaries are established between those who know and those who do not know. Those closest to the problem look for someone or something to blame as they struggle to explain to themselves what has happened. They come to terms with the problem by developing an acceptable rationale, which may or may not be accurate. When inaccurate, it leads to poor decisions because some of the necessary ingredients for good decision making are omitted. There may not have been enough information to make an informed decision. All relevant facts may not have been sought. Enough stakeholders may not have been involved in the decision-making process. Or, the search for all possible alternatives may have been stopped prematurely. When the decision reached is a poor one, the organization has not been well served. Although poor decisions stop the decline temporarily, they only postpone the continuation of the downward spiral. When not stopped, the organization continues in decline until the downward spiral reaches the bottom. At the bottom there are only two choices: to let the firm dissolve or to rebuild it.

Decline can be dealt with ineffectively as well as effectively. Dysfunctional ways of dealing with decline take varying forms, ranging from total oblivion to denial to shortsighted attempts to fix the symptoms without treating the cause of the problem. The functional way to deal with decline is to directly confront it—to recognize it as something important that has to be dealt with as quickly and as thoroughly as possible. The appropriate strategy must be chosen and implemented. After the strategies are in operation, the job is not finished. It is as important to monitor and adjust the corrective maneuvers as it is to make them in the first place. New strategies are only successful at promoting the turnaround when they work as anticipated. Often the best made plans require revision. As the organization moves upward in the renewal process, strategies need to be adjusted to make them fit improving circumstances.

There are visible signs of decline that serve as signposts on an organization's downward path. Early in the declination trend economic and subjective benchmarks denote early warning signs of impending trouble. Declining market share, declining resources, unclear priorities, loss of direction, absence of long-range planning, pervasive employee discontent, increased absenteeism, unusually high personnel turnover rates, negative coverage in the media, and too little information coming in through formal and informal channels are a few indicators. When not heeded early, much later these benchmarks fit together as pieces in a puzzle to help explain why decline occurred, when it started, and what form it took.

Some organizations find themselves in decline because of their inability to foresee and adapt to uncontrollable changes in the environment. As a company evolves and matures, downturns in the economy and increased competition in the marketplace affect the company's overall performance. Business cycles and consumer demands change. Changes in regulatory policies and increases in costs of production affect performance. The question managers must continually ask is whether a downturn is a routine seasonal fluctuation or is symptomatic of a situation far more threatening to the long-term vitality of the organization. For all the controllable reasons of decline, the uncontrollable phenomena of change and chance still play a part. The late 1980s brought with them a confusing economic outlook. Rather than an overall recession, there were sector-specific recessions. As farming and oil production were doing poorly, information industries and high technology firms were thriving. As manufacturing was struggling to get back on its feet, service industries flourished. The economic condition of the 1990s will continue to mirror a labile transition from a manufacturing economy to a service and information economy.

The public and nonprofit sectors of the economy are not immune to uncontrollable change. The growing federal deficit and changing relationships between the federal, state, and local governments affect public agencies and the services they provide. Likewise a changing philosophy about what services the government should provide causes public agencies to continually reassess their mission. The 1980s introduced a growing acceptance of privatization. This was manifested by enforcement of the federal government's contracting out policy, which requires that services that private firms are willing to provide should be opened to competitive bidding. If private firms can provide the services with equal reliability but substantially lower costs than government, then they are granted the right to do so. Changes in public willingness or capability to donate funds to charitable organizations contribute to the list of uncontrollable changes that govern the health of voluntary agencies. So all sectors of the economy are affected by changes over which they have little control.

The bottoming out process, when handled successfully, marks the point at which the downward spiral stops and the upward climb begins. It is the point at which a realistic appraisal is made of the problem and its causes, and constructive action is taken. It is during this phase that the organization's culture is in a real squeeze. The most constructive aspects must be safeguarded and nurtured. The dysfunctional segments, especially those that contributed to the decline, must be removed. Even the most optimistic among those leading a revitalization effort cannot help but feel discouraged at some point in the turnaround process. Change does not come easily to people. Although there will be a few committed to the change, and some willing to go along with it, there will always be some who resent it. When a change is introduced, people are being expected to alter the way they have been doing their work. Since it is easier to continue doing what one is accustomed to, breaking the habit and replacing it with a new one is resisted. It is difficult to bring an organization's personnel to the awareness that the company is in dire jeopardy without so threatening them that they become paralyzed by fear of losing their jobs. The vitality of the culture and the skills of leadership are truly tested at this point. People feel threatened with impending changes and worry about losing their status or even their jobs.

An organizational culture develops an equilibrium over time. As a consequence, to change one aspect of a culture is to produce unintended changes in other parts of the culture. Norms, values, traditions, and acceptable ways of behaving, accommodate to one another and develop as a whole. Metanorms reinforce the corporate culture and the status quo. Informal sanctions reward those who comply with cultural norms and to punish those who thwart accepted standards. Changing one norm has a ripple effect throughout the culture. For example, if the organization has developed an informal norm that closing the shop early on Fridays is acceptable, then it will take more than a memorandum posted on the bulletin board to pass the word that what was previously sanctioned is no longer acceptable. With that change will come complaints that "we've always closed the shop early. Why should we stop now?" Questions about what other traditions are about to change will erupt and the rumor mill will hum with speculation. For this reason, to introduce change in one aspect is to, ipso facto, introduce change in other, seemingly unrelated, aspects of how people go about doing their work.

Renewal occurs in stages, and although it must be pursued

vigorously, it takes time and progresses through predictable phases. Just as characteristics endure through decline, there are characteristics that endure through the revitalization process. Beginning with commitment from the top of the organization, activity is motivated by a desire to see positive results. A period of strategy and consensus building follows. As new strategies are planned and agreed upon and communicated through the work force, implementation occurs.

The infrastructure of an organization is the bricks and mortar, equipment, communication channels, classification and compensation system, policy and procedure manuals, and so forth. These parts of an organization are the easiest and most obvious things to change. When a change is made, its effect is tangible. From a symbolic standpoint, this is a good starting point to make the renewal obvious to everyone and to signal the recovery. However, it is the "people infrastructure" that will produce long lasting effects. Not until the work force buys in to the recovery efforts, will the mechanical infrastructure be used constructively by it. The people infrastructure has to be in place before the mechanical infrastructure will hold together and have the desired effect over the long run. This means placing influential opinion shapers throughout the organization so that they reach and influence as many of the workers as possible. The opinion shapers throughout the organization need to be enlisted into the renewal effort so they know what is going on, why it is happening, and how they fit into the picture. Through word-of-mouth communication with their peers, information as well as a positive attitude must be transmitted. The final step of the renewal process is that new behaviors are practiced and cemented into place to replace old habits.

LESSONS TO BE LEARNED FROM THE PHOENIX SYNDROME

How does knowing about the stages of decline and renewal help today's manager who is struggling to succeed? The answer to this question is that it helps the manager to recognize what is happening and to look into the future and predict what is coming. Being forewarned of future events arms the astute manager with the ability to foresee further decline and initiate revitalization efforts early in the downswing. Being able to leapfrog future stages of decline requires identifying the current status of the organization. Once the current condition of the organization is known, it is relatively easy to predict the stages that loom ahead. When sighted far enough in advance, strategies can be devised for avoiding them. By so doing, the company is launched into a recovery mode far sooner than would otherwise be the case. Leapfrogging additional stages of decline can only occur when the leadership of the organization is skilled enough not only to look ahead but to look at the organization today and understand what the signals are telling. Interpreting and acting on the signals requires leadership, regular reevaluation of the link between organizational goals and procedures for meeting them, and an accurate reading of the environment.

There is one warning that should hang on every manager's wall as a constant reminder. It is to listen to what those inside as well as those outside the organization are saying. It is critical to actively listen to what employees and clients say, as well as to hear what is not being said. Communication channels must be kept open and information must flow freely. Although rumors may be mostly wrong in their content, they bear watching. Regardless of their accuracy, they warn the listener of concerns among the workers and foretell of problems just beginning to take shape. Rarely will a rumor that is *totally* unfounded be passed around.

Active listening is a skill easily ignored. Astute managers know it is an invaluable aid, however. It involves listening carefully to what is being said and being certain to verify that the listener heard what the speaker said. This is to assume that the listener receives the message the speaker intends to send. Far too often, people listen to what others say and interpret the message in terms of what the listener already thinks is the case. With perceptual blinders, the message gets lost amidst the listener's preconceived notions.

Are the stages of the Phoenix Syndrome carved in stone and inviolable? No. In fact, the stages often will be superimposed upon one another, seeming to appear simultaneously rather than sequentially. Sometimes one stage will have such an impact that it will overshadow others and draw attention to itself and its consequences. All in all, however, the metaphor largely mirrors reality. Although organizations and the people who staff them differ from one another, there are commonalities that produce similar consequences regardless of where the problems arise.

Can U.S. companies move beyond this metaphor? Yes, for it only requires an astute, timely observation of the organization, what is happening within it, and what is happening outside it. But the next question is, will U.S. firms learn from current problems so they do not have to go into the Phoenix Syndrome? Probably not. The future of the U.S. economy is not as promising as it was twenty years ago. From the standpoint of the national economy, the U.S. is stumbling at its attempts to renew itself and change from a leading manufacturing nation to a leading provider of services and information. How close it will come to succeeding is an unanswered question. It is possible for U.S. firms to climb the staircase of renewal, but first a willingness to resist taking the path of least resistance is required. The United States is a nation that wants protection from foreign competition rather than open competition. It is the nation that wants to stop the importation of drugs rather than deal with the values that give rise to drug abuse. The work force appears to be setting aside the fabled Horatio Alger myth that encouraged each worker to rely on self-discipline to overcome problems. The United States as a country dismisses blame; likewise, workers point fingers of blame away from themselves, looking for someone, some company, or some nation to blame for their troubles. The easy fix is the path of least resistance and requires the fewest changes in behavior. But it is the easy fix, the thumb in the dike that does little to stop the damage in the long run.

The adversarial relationship between labor and management has severely eroded the pride individuals take in producing their work. Rather than working together to produce quality products, both labor and management are reduced to trying to get the most out of their adversary. A sense of working together so laborers produce their best effort, and are proud of it, along with the organization's having received the work force's best effort is a win-win proposition. When workers believe they are being taken advantage of, and organizations believe that workers do not care about their work, there is no reason to expect that American products will improve in quality, that people will take more pride in where they work, or that companies will take more pride in the labor force. Self-discipline within the labor force and pride in the product are key ingredients to insuring quality workmanship. No amount of external controls, such as rules and penalties, can do a better job of conscientiously monitoring an organization's output.

Tomorrow's organizations, and their work forces, represent the future of the nation's economy. Organizations are complex because the people who staff them are complex. To try to understand only one side of the issue, organization versus work force, is to artificially divide subjects that have to be discussed together to be meaningful. Organizations are created by people to serve the needs of people. They are staffed by people who are charged with accomplishing the goals people have set. Although signs of an organization's health can be checked by looking at production levels and profit margins, the whole organization cannot be known until the people within it are taken into consideration. If managing were as easy as watching the bottom line dollar figures, there would be no need for managers. Accountants could run organizations.

Of seven forces for renewal inherent in any organization, only two of the seven represent non-people oriented forces, and those two rely on people for their effectiveness. Clear goals, leadership, open channels of communication, can-do culture, up-to-date technology, adaptability, and reorganization or merger, are the forces. Goals are set by people for people. Leadership is a human quality. Open channels of communication rely on people using them. The culture is the human culture, created by intermingling and informal friendship networks of all the people who work for the company. Up-to-date technology is only as good as the people who operate the equipment. Adaptability is a human trait manifested in an attitude. Reorganization and merger must be decided by people and implemented by people.

Although markets are international and demands for service are dynamic, human behavior is pretty much the same as it has always been. Human decision making is at the center of work, regardless of how technologically sophisticated a task is. It is decisions made that point toward the path the organization will travel. Decision making is critical. Good decision making requires recognizing which decisions are necessary to be made. At the point when one determines that action must be taken, the first consideration is what sort of action. This requires a review of the issues at hand. The second step is choosing who is going to make them. Whether a decision should be made by one person or a team, by top management or a department head, by consensus or by decree, are all considerations necessary to insure that the decision will be the right one, made by the best people to make it. The next step is to determine the goal that is to be achieved by a decision. If it is to maximize profit it requires one set of factors. If it is to maximize productivity within one department, it requires a different set of factors. The next is to identify what resources are necessary to achieve the goals and objectives. Then skills required to achieve the goals and objectives must be defined. Then an inventory of the skills of present staff is useful. This is certainly true when staff reductions are being considered. It may be that current staff have the necessary skills but that they have been prohibited from exercising them under the past structure. Next, several workable options for achieving each of the goals should be developed so that a choice can be made after considering the costs and benefits of each. Of course, the final step is to make the decision and implement it in ways that are fair and will produce the desired result. Expert systems are computer software programs that mirror the decision-making processes an expert uses to solve a problem. They are built by interviewing the experts who make the decisions and encoding the steps they go through. An expert system does not create a decision that is better than a person can make. It does cause the decision-making process to be more consistent across people and conditions. Decision making can be aided by an expert system program, but it cannot be replaced. An efficient use of technology provides a force for renewal—but only after the personnel involved are convinced that they want the new technology.

Proactive management is essential for turning an organization around, in contradiction to reactive management, otherwise called managing by exception. The former relies upon forward thinking management that keeps abreast of the organization's performance and monitors and acts upon forecasts. The latter, management by exception, assumes a passive stance. Not until something is broken is it fixed. The break is the exception and it is only repaired when the break is apparent. Although this is an efficient way to use management in a stable environment with a steady market, it misses the mark in a rapidly changing environment. It is management by exception that allows dysfunctional procedures to continue long after their useful life has expired. It is management by exception that assumes that the way operations are conducted are as effective for tomorrow as they were for yesterday. An organization that is complacent is doomed to suffer decline and have great difficulty resurrecting itself.

Organizations of tomorrow must demand self-discipline of personnel and an internalized focus on quality. It should be employees, not consumers, who bring defective materials and workmanship to the attention of management. Proactive management will succeed at this, while reactive management will fail. In an era of quick fixes and quick profits, quality improvement and productivity improvement efforts have an uphill battle. Reactive management responds to problems but only at the point at which a problem is identified. It supervises the ongoing operation. Proactive, on the other hand, leads.

Double loop learning is part of proactive managing. Rather than focusing only on the problem, fixing it, and going blindly forward, other aspects must be considered as well. Management must attend not only to what is wrong but also to what is right. That is, that which is wrong must be corrected, but that which is right must be reinforced and rewarded to prevent problems from receiving too much attention at the expense of the strengths. This is contrary to the customary way of simply looking for problems and attending to them. When problems receive all the attention and strengths are ignored, then it is not until the strengths diminish and become problems that attention is focused on them.

Although technology has made great strides, human nature and human passions have not changed much since long before Shakespeare depicted them in his plays. Organizational structures, reporting channels, and job descriptions are like boxes superimposed over people to constrain their outreach and regularize their influence on other parts of the organization. But people do not do well segmenting their lives, interests, and passions. A more fluid system for organizing people and structuring their work is necessary for two reasons. It allows each individual to grow on the job and it allows the organization to extract the individual's best effort for its own purposes. An organization should have as an operational goal that all employees give their best effort to the organization so it, in turn, achieves its best output. Implicit within this goal is an awareness of the exchange relationship between employer and employees. In return for employees' contributing their best effort, sufficient meaningful inducements are required. In exchange for contributing their best, the organization must provide not only salary but also higher order needs fulfillment, including status, self-esteem, a sense of accomplishment and fulfillment, and affiliation with an organization of which they are proud.

It is a rare organization that does not have interested, motivated people standing ready to help bring about a revitalization. Its work force is the greatest impetus for renewal on which an organization in decline can rely. Harnessing the energy and optimism and motivation of these people makes the difference between introducing patchwork strategies and putting lasting, successful new procedures in place.

Bibliography

Aaker, David A., & Mascarenhas, Briance. 1984. The need for strategic flexibility. *Journal of Business Strategy, 5,* 74-82.

Ackerman, Laurence D. 1984. The psychology of corporation: how identity influences business. *Journal of Business Strategy, 5*(1), 56-65.

Albrecht, Terrance L., & Ropp, Vickie A. 1984. Communicating about innovation in networks of three U.S. organizations. *Journal of Communication, 34,* 78-91.

Altman, Edward I. 1983. *Corporate Financial Distress.* New York: John Wiley & Sons.

Argyris, Chris. 1980. Making the undiscussable and its undiscussability discussable. *Public Administration Review, 40,* 205-213.

Associated Press. 1986a, August 1. O ring seals missed 3 safety inspections. *Birmingham Post-Herald,* p. A10.

Associated Press. 1986b, July 29. Cost-cutting plan causes Kodak to lose $12.2 million. *Birmingham Post-Herald,* p. C3.

Associated Press. 1986c, July 2. CBS plans "painful" paring of as many as 600 jobs. *Birmingham Post-Herald,* p. E4.

Associated Press. 1986d, May 17. Commission checking report Marshall records destroyed. *Birmingham Post-Herald,* p. A10.

Aviation Week & Space Technology. 1987a, December 14. NASA seeks to block massive reductions in station budget, p. 29.

Aviation Week & Space Technology. 1987b, December 7. NASA selects station contractors despite funding uncertainties, pp. 18-19.

Aviation Week & Space Technology. 1987c, March 9. Task force urges NASA to adopt manned Mars goal, p. 263.

Aviation Week & Space Technology. 1986a, December 22. Kennedy photo analysts review Challenger videos, p. 27.

Aviation Week & Space Technology. 1986b, November 17. Transcript reveals launch controllers waived Challenger temperature warnings, pp. 51-52.

Aviation Week & Space Technology. 1986c, November 10. Shuttle management revamped to resemble that of Apollo, pp. 30-31.

Aviation Week & Space Technology. 1986d, August 11. NASA, contractors may lay off 25,000 if 1987 budget shortfall is severe, p. 24.

Aviation Week & Space Technology. 1986e, July 14, NASA establishes safety office at headquarters, p. 32.

Aviation Week & Space Technology. 1986f, June 9. NASA's fiscal 1987 budget continues in disarray, p. 17.

Aviation Week & Space Technology. 1986g, February 17. NASA assesses external tank's role in Challenger accident, pp. 18-20.

Aviation Week & Space Technology. 1986h, February 10. Booster investigation forces examination of procedures by NASA and contractors, pp. 23-24.

Aviation Week & Space Technology. 1967, April 17. Board reports on Apollo fire investigation, pp. 100-114.

Bainbrigge, Marion S. 1969. *A Walk in Other Worlds with Dante.* Port Washington, N.Y.: Kennikat Press.

Beggs, James M. 1985, July 8. NASA's productivity and quality enhancement program. *Design News,* pp. 37-56.

Bernstein, Aaron, & Garland, Susan B. 1987, November 9. The AFL-CIO: A tougher team with the teamsters. *Business Week,* p. 110.

Bhide, Amar. 1986. Hustle as strategy. *Harvard Business Review,* 64(5), 59-65.

Blakely, Steve. 1986, April 5. Space program faces costly, clouded future. *Congressional Quarterly,* pp. 731-735.

Branst, Lee. 1984, February. Disneyland—a kingdom of service quality. *Quality,* pp. 16-18.

Brinkley, John. 1986, June 13. Charges flung at NASA headquarters. *Birmingham Post-Herald,* p. A8.

Brown, James K. (Ed.) 1984. *Manufacturing: New Concepts and New Technology to Meet New Competition.* New York: The Conference Board, Inc.

Brown, James K., & Elvers, Lita M. 1983. *Research & Development: Key Issues for Management.* New York: The Conference Board.

Brown, James K., & Kay, Lillian W. (Eds.) 1985. *Corporate R&D Strategy, Innovation and Funding Issues.* New York: The Conference Board, Inc.

Bryan, John H., Jr. 1984. Managing Change. Address made to the 1984 President's Meeting, unpublished.

Business Quarterly. 1982, December. Fear of change: the great immobilizer, p. 33.

Business Week. 1986a, August 18. Is Eastern giving Lorenzo a lesson in cost-cutting? p. 39.

Business Week. 1986b, March 10. Scherer is ready to try new medicine, pp. 58-62.

Business Week. 1985, March 22. Hospital chains struggle to stay in the pink, pp. 258-259.

Business Week. 1984a, November 5. Who's excellent now? pp. 76-88.

Business Week. 1984b, November 5. A shaken caterpillar retools to take on a more competitive world, pp. 91-94.

Business Week. 1984c, March 12. Problems in Walt Disney's magic kingdom, pp. 50-54.

Business Week. 1984d, March 12. Deere: Quality problems show up after a bad bet on the economy, pp. 61-62.

Bylinsky, Gene. 1984, May 29. America's best-managed factories. *Fortune,* pp. 16-24.

Cameron, Kim, Kim, Myung U., & Whetten, David A. 1987. Organizational effects of decline and turbulence. *Administrative Science Quarterly, 32,* 222-240.

Cameron, Kim, & Zammuto, Raymond. 1983. Matching managerial strategies to conditions of decline. *Human Resource Management, 22*(4), 359-375.

Carnegie Forum on Education and the Economy. 1986. *A Nation Prepared: Teachers for the 21st Century.* Available from: Carnegie Forum on Education and the Economy, P.O. Box 157, Hyattsville, Md. 20781.

Chaffee, Ellen Earle. 1985. Three models of strategy. *Academy of Management Review, 10*(1), 89-98.

Clarke, Clifford J. 1983. The end of bureaucratization? Recent trends in cross-national evidence. *Social Science Quarterly, 64,* 127-135.

Contino, R., & Lorusso, R. M. 1982. The theory Z turnaround of a public agency. *Public Administration Review, 42,* 66-72.

Cook, Richard. 1986a, November. The Rogers Commission failed. *The Washington Monthly,* pp. 13-21.

Cook, Richard. 1986b, March 16. Why I blew the whistle on NASA's O-ring woes. *The Washington Post,* pp. D1-D2.

Cooper, Henry S. F., Jr. 1976. *A House in Space.* London: Angus & Robertson, Ltd.

Cornett, Harris. 1984. *Acts of desperation during decline and metamorphosis.* Unpublished manuscript.

Corrigan, Richard. 1986a, March 22. NASA's midlife crisis. *National Journal,* pp. 686-692.

Corrigan, Richard. 1986b, March 15. Pressure to launch. *National Journal,* p. 674.

Corrigan, Richard. 1986c, February 15. Eclipsing NASA. *National Journal,* p. 421.

Covault, Craig. 1988, January 18. President signs space policy backing lunar, Mars course. *Aviation Week & Space Technology,* pp. 14-16.

Covault, Craig. 1987, March 9. Reagan to consider additional funding for station program. *Aviation Week & Space Technology,* pp. 260-261.

Covault, Craig. 1985, November 25. New deep-space explorations tied to 1986 Shuttle schedule. *Aviation Week & Space Technology,* pp. 18-19.

Covault, Craig. 1983, March 7. New Challenger engine cracks found. *Aviation Week & Space Technology,* pp. 23-25.

Covault, Craig. 1979, October 15. Shuttle aborts pose new challenges. *Aviation Week & Space Technology,* pp. 39-45.

Cummings, T. G., Blumenthal, J. F., & Greiner, L. E. 1983. Managing organizational decline: the case for transorganizational systems. *Human Resource Management, 22*(4), 377-390.

Dalton, G. W., Lawrence, P. R., & Greiner, L. E. 1970. *Organizational Change and Development.* Homewood, Ill.: Irwin.

Damanpour, Fariborz, & Evan, William M. 1984. Organizational innovation and performance: the problem of "organizational lag." *Administrative Science Quarterly, 29,* 392-409.

Deal, Terrence E., & Kennedy, Allan A. 1982. *Corporate Cultures.* Reading, Mass.: Addison-Wesley Publishing Co.

Deveny, Kathleen. 1986, December 8. Thinking ahead got Deere in big trouble. *Business Week*, p. 69.

Doherty, Richard. 1986, March 31. NASA to restore 3,000 sensors to shuttle. *Electronic Engineering Times*, pp. 12-13.

Dopp, Darren. 1986, August 10. She turns Hudson River port into moneymaker. *Birmingham News*, p. 4D.

Dorr, Les, Jr. 1986, January. Going with the flow. *Space World*, pp. 26-29.

Douglas, William O. 1987. *The Douglas Letters*. Bethesda, Md.: Adler & Adler, Publishers, Inc.

Drucker, Peter F. 1988. The coming of the new organization. *Harvard Business Review, 66*(1), 45-53.

Drucker, Peter F. 1985, May-June. The discipline of innovation. *Harvard Business Review*, 67-72.

Dunnavant, Robert. 1986, August 10. Phones at 'Whistle-blower Central' keep NASA gadfly Bush hopping. *Birmingham News*, p. 4A.

Durham, J. W., & Smith, H. L. 1982. Toward a general theory of organizational deterioration. *Administration & Society, 14*, 373-400.

The Economist. 1984, December 22. Managing corporate change. *293*, 95-96.

Engardio, Pete. 1987, October 12. Why Eastern is backing off from a union showdown. *Business Week*, pp. 108-109.

Ertel, Ivan D., & Newkirk, Roland W., with Brooks, Courtney G. 1978. *The Apollo Spacecraft*. Washington, D.C.: National Aeronautics and Space Administration.

Fanning, David (Producer), & Wiley, Lou (Ed.) 1984, January 16. Crisis at general hospital (Television show on *Frontline*, PBS). WGBH Transcripts, 125 Western Avenue, Boston, Mass. 02134.

Fink, Donald E. 1987, February 2. NASA under siege. *Aviation Week & Space Technology*, p. 11.

Fink, Donald E. 1986, February 17. Missed opportunities. . . . *Aviation Week & Space Technology*, p. 13.

Finkin, Eugene F. 1985. Company turnaround. *Journal of Business Strategy, 5*(4), 14-24.

Fisher, Anne B. 1985, August 5. Coke's brand-loyalty lesson. *Fortune*, pp. 44-46.

Flax, Steven. 1985, January 7. Can Chrysler keep rolling along? *Fortune*, pp. 34-39.

Foley, Theresa M. 1988, January 4. Congress directs NASA to adapt space station to shrinking budget. *Aviation Week & Space Technology*, pp. 32-33.

Foley, Theresa M. 1986, November 17. NASA takes action to rebuild safety, quality assurance. *Aviation Week & Space Technology*, pp. 49-52.

Ford, Jeffrey. 1980. The occurrence of structural hysteresis in declining organizations. *Academy of Management Review, 5*, 589-598.

Fortune. 1986a, September 29. Airline turbulence spreads across the land, p. 6.

Fortune. 1986b, July 7. A pioneering airline C.E.O. looks ahead, p. 53.

Freeman, John. 1982. Organizational life cycles and natural selection processes. In B. M. Staw and L. L. Cumming (Eds.), *Research in Organizational Behavior, 4*, 1-32. Greenwich, Conn.: JAI Press.

Freeman, John, Carroll, Glenn R., & Hannan, Michael T. 1983. The liability of newness: age dependence in organizational death rates. *American Sociological Review, 48*, 692-710.

Gaertner, Gregory H., Gaertner, Karen N., & Devine, Irene. 1983. Federal agencies in the context of transition: a contrast between democratic and organizational theories. *Public Administration Review, 43,* 421-432.

Galbraith, Jay. 1973. *Designing Complex Organizations.* Reading, Mass.: Addison-Wesley.

Gardner, Meryl P. 1985. Creating a corporate culture for the eighties. *Business Horizons, 28*(1), 59-63.

Gay, Lance. 1985, September 3. Unions try to change image, work on different approach. *Birmingham Post-Herald,* p. C1.

Gilbert, Nick. 1986, July. Unhitch the tractor, sunshine. *Euromoney,* pp. 27-33.

Gilder, George. 1984. *The Spirit of Enterprise.* New York: Simon and Schuster.

Gilmore, Thomas, & Hirschhorn, Larry. 1983. Management challenges under conditions of retrenchment. *Human Resource Management, 22*(4), 341-357.

Giroux, Gary, & Wiggins, Casper E., Jr. 1983, December. Chapter XI and corporate resuscitation. *Financial Executive, 51,* 37-41.

Gluck, Frederick W. 1985. ''Big bang'' management. *Journal of Business Strategy, 6*(1), 59-64.

Government Computer News. 1986, July 4. Firm escapes extinction with renewed DBMS focus, p. 57.

Greenhalgh, Leonard. 1982. Maintaining organizational effectiveness during organizational retrenchment. *Journal of Applied Behavioral Science, 18*(2), 155-170.

Greenhalgh, Leonard, & Rosenblatt, Zehava. 1984. Job insecurity: toward conceptual clarity. *Academy of Management Review, 9*(3), 438-448.

Guy, Mary E. 1985. *Professionals in Organizations: Debunking a Myth.* New York: Praeger.

Hacker, Barton C., & Grimwood, James M. 1977. *On the Shoulders of Titans.* Washington, D.C.: National Aeronautics and Space Administration.

Hampton, William J. 1987, October 5. Why Chrysler can't afford to go off it's diet. *Business Week,* p. 84.

Hampton, William J., with Rossant, John. 1987, March 23. Now, for Chrysler's next trick. . . . *Business Week,* pp. 32-33.

Harrigan, Kathryn R. 1984, Winter. Managing declining businesses. *Journal of Business Strategy, 4,* 74-78.

Harrigan, Kathryn R. 1982. Strategic planning for endgame. *Long Range Planning, 15*(6), 45-48.

Harrigan, Kathryn R. 1980. *Strategies for Declining Businesses.* Lexington, Mass.: D.C. Heath and Company.

Hayes, Robert H. 1985. Strategic planning—forward in reverse? *Harvard Business Review, 63*(6), 111-119.

Hays, Richard D. 1985. The myth and reality of supervisory development. *Business Horizons, 28*(1), 75-79.

Heany, Donald F. 1985. Businesses in profit trouble. *Journal of Business Strategy, 5*(4), 4-12.

Hector, Gary. 1985, April 1. More than mortgages ails Bankamerica. *Fortune,* pp. 50-62.

Higgins, Richard G., Jr. 1984. Strategies for management of decline and productivity improvement in local government. *Public Productivity Review, 8*(4), 332-352.

Hirschman, Albert O. 1970. *Exit, Voice, and Loyalty.* Cambridge, Mass.: Harvard University Press.

Holusha, John. 1986, December 7. Advice for Detroit's humbled giant. *New York Times,* pp. 1F, 32F.

Horovitz, Jacques. 1984, Winter. New perspectives on strategic management. *Journal of Business Strategy, 4,* 19-33.

Hotz, Robert. 1988, January 5. NASA lagging in shuttle safety, report finds. *The Atlanta Constitution,* p. 1A.

Hurst, David K. 1984, May-June. Of boxes, bubbles, and effective management. *Harvard Business Review, 62,* pp. 78-88.

Iacocca, Lee A. 1983. The rescue and resuscitation of Chrysler. *Journal of Business Strategy, 4*(1), 67-69.

Industry Week. 1982, November 15. Management rapped for bankruptcy woes, pp. 79, 83.

Janis, Irving L. 1982. *Groupthink* (2d edition). Boston: Houghton Mifflin Co.

Janis, Irving L. 1972. *Victims of Groupthink.* Boston: Houghton Mifflin Co.

Kanter, Rosabeth Moss. 1983. *The Change Masters.* New York: Simon & Schuster, Inc.

Kanter, Rosabeth Moss, & Stein, Barry A. (Eds.) 1979. *Life in Organizations.* New York: Basic Books, Inc.

Kaufman, Herbert. 1985. *Time, Chance, and Organizations.* Chatham, N.J.: Chatham House Publishers, Inc.

Kaufman, Herbert. 1971. *The Limits of Organizational Change.* University, Ala.: The University of Alabama Press.

Kerchner, Charles T. 1984. Shortages and gluts of public school teachers: there must be a policy problem here somewhere. *Public Administration Review, 44,* 292-298.

Ketchum, Robert H. 1982, November-December. Retrenchment: the uses and misuses of LIFO in downsizing an organization. *Personnel, 59,* 25-30.

Kiechel, Walter, III. 1982. Corporate strategists under fire. *Fortune, 106*(13), 34-39.

Kilpatrick, Andrew. 1986, October 16. Surprise came despite taste tests, Coke exec says. *Birmingham Post-Herald,* p. A9.

Kimberly, John R., Miles, Robert H., & Associates. 1980. *The Organizational Life Cycle: Issues in the Creation, Transformation, and Decline of Organizations.* San Francisco, Calif.: Jossey-Bass, Inc.

King, Laura. 1986, May 7. Associated Press wire service report on NASA's quality control, no title, no. 2358.

Kloman, Erasmus. 1986. Preface to *Nasa: the Vision and the Reality.* Washington, D.C.: National Academy of Public Administration.

Kloman, Erasmus. 1985. *Nasa: the Vision and the Reality.* Washington, D.C.: National Academy of Public Administration.

Koepp, Stephen. 1986, October 27. Feeling the crunch from foreign chips. *Time,* pp. 72-73.

Kolcum, Edward H. 1987, January 12. NASA to begin rebonding Discovery tiles. *Aviation Week & Space Technology,* p. 105.

Koontz, Harold, & O'Donnell, Cyril. 1978. *Essentials of Management.* New York: McGraw-Hill Book Co.

Kruglanski, Arie W. 1986, August. Freeze-think and the Challenger. *Psychology Today,* pp. 48-49.

Labich, Kenneth. 1984, April 30. Monsanto's brave new world. *Fortune*, pp. 59-68.

Lappen, Alyssa A. 1987. Back in focus. *Forbes, 140*(4), 8.

Ledford, Gerald E., Jr., & Lawler, Edward E., III. 1982. Quality of worklife programs, coordination, and productivity. *Journal of Contemporary Business, 11*(2), 93-106.

Legislative Audit Council of the State of South Carolina General Assembly. 1983, November 16. *A Management and Performance Review of the South Carolina Department of Mental Health.* Columbia, S.C.: author.

Levine, Arnold S. 1982. *Managing NASA in the Apollo Era.* Washington, D.C.: National Aeronautics and Space Administration.

Levine, Charles H. 1985. Retrenchment, human resource erosion, and the role of the personnel manager. *Public Personnel Management Journal, 13,* pp. 249-263.

Levson, Elizabeth, & Guy, Mary E. 1987. Information channels for critical care nurses. *Dimensions of Critical Care Nursing, 6*(1), 40-46.

Lorange, Peter, & Nelson, Robert T. 1987. How to recognize—and avoid—organizational decline. *Sloan Management Review, 28*(3), 41-48.

MacNeil/Lehrer NewsHour. 1986, June 9. Report on Disaster. Transcript No. 2791. Educational Broadcasting Corp. and GWETA, Box 345, New York, N.Y. 10101.

Magnuson, Ed. 1986, February 10. "They slipped the surly bonds of earth to touch the face of God." *Time*, pp. 24-31.

Main, Jeremy. 1984, April 2. The trouble with managing Japanese-style. *Fortune*, pp. 42-50.

Mann, David S., & Carter, Luther F. 1986. Exploring the policy formulation and implementation linkage: NASA and the Challenger. Paper presented at the Annual Meeting of the Southern Political Science Association, November 6-8, 1986 in Atlanta, Georgia.

Marcial, Gene G. 1986, June 30. Fish oil helps Scherer get healthy. *Business Week*, p. 58.

Marinucci, Carla. 1986, August 7. Hot ads fight cooler wars as bottlers expand territory. *Birmingham Post-Herald*, p. B8.

Marwood, D. C. L. 1985. ICL: Crisis and swift recovery. *Long Range Planning, 18*(2), 10-21.

Mateja, James. 1985, September 22. Iacocca plans: 'Laugh all the way to the bank.' *Birmingham News*, p. 8B.

Mauss, Armand L. 1982. Salvation and survival on skid row: a comment on Rooney. *Social Forces, 60,* 898-904.

McCann, Thomas. 1976. *An American Company: The Tragedy of United Fruit.* New York: Crown.

McComas, Maggie. 1985, June 10. Quaker is feeling its oats. *Fortune*, pp. 54-64.

McDougall, Walter A. 1985. *The Heavens and the Earth.* New York: Basic Books.

McGinnis, Michael A., & Ackelsberg, M. Robert. 1983. Effective innovation management: missing link in strategic planning? *Journal of Business Strategy, 4*(1), 59-66.

McKelvey, Bill, & Aldrich, Howard. 1983. Populations, natural selection, and applied organizational science. *Administrative Science Quarterly, 28,* 101-128.

Mendleson, Jack L., & Golen, Steven P. 1985. Achieving credibility as a manager. *Industrial Management, 27*(3), 16-17.

Merwin, John. 1987. Not in the next 30 days. *Forbes, 140*(1), 72-80.

Miles, Robert H. 1982. *Coffin Nails and Corporate Strategies.* Englewood Cliffs, N.J.: Prentice-Hall.

Mintzberg, Henry. 1979. *The Structuring of Organizations.* Englewood Cliffs, N.J.: Prentice-Hall.

Mohrman, Susan A., & Mohrman, A. M., Jr. 1983. Employee involvement in declining organizations. *Human Resource Management, 22*(4), 445-465.

Molotsky, Irvin. 1986, February 19. Drug makers stick to using capsules. *New York Times, 135,* pp. 1, 13.

Moskowitz, Milton R. 1984, Spring. Company performance roundup. *Business and Society Review, 49,* 65-71.

Murray, V. V., & Jick, T. D. 1985. Taking stock of organizational decline management: some issues and illustrations from an empirical study. *Journal of Management, 11,* 111-123.

Narayanan, V. K., & Nath, Raghu. 1984. The influence of group cohesiveness on some changes induced by flexitime: a quasi-experiment. *Journal of Applied Behavioral Science, 20,* 265-276.

National Academy of Public Administration. June 1977. *U.S. Transportation in the 1980's: Organizational Alternatives.* Washington, D.C.: National Academy of Public Administration.

National Commission on Excellence in Education. 1983. *A Nation at Risk: The Imperative for Educational Reform.* Washington, D.C.: U.S. Government Printing Office.

National Journal. 1986, March 15. A cheaper shot, p. 619.

National Journal. 1970, January 17. Nixon administration announces plans for another reduction in space spending, pp. 25-26.

National Petroleum News. 1987, April. Texaco's image to benefit from Kinnear's management, pp. 72-73.

Neustadt, Richard E., & Fineberg, Harvey V. 1978. The Swine Flu Affair. Washington, D.C.: U.S. Government Printing Office, pp. 1-30. Reprinted in Richard J. Stillman II, 1984, *Public Administration.* Boston: Houghton Mifflin.

Newsweek. 1970a, June 29. Apollo 13: the culprits, p. 57.

Newsweek. 1970b, June 15. Apollo 13: the reason why, p. 61.

Newsweek. 1967a, March 13. Death by miscalculation, p. 94.

Newsweek. 1967b, February 6. 'Fire in the space craft,' pp. 25-29.

Norman, David A. 1985. Success strategy for rapid growth. *Industrial Management. 27*(4), 1-4.

Normyle, William J. 1967a, April 17. NASA implements board findings. *Aviation Week & Space Technology,* pp. 26-30.

Normyle, William J. 1967b, April 10. NASA shifts key Apollo officials. *Aviation Week & Space Technology,* p. 26.

Nulty, Peter. 1985, May 27. The case for shrinking Mobil Corporation. *Fortune,* pp. 42-50.

Nystrom, Paul C., & Starbuck, W. H. 1984, Spring. To avoid organizational crises, unlearn. *Organizational Dynamics, 12,* 53-65.

O'Reilly, Brian. 1985, July 8. Texas Instruments: new boss, big job. *Fortune,* pp. 60-64.

Ouchi, William G. 1982. Theory Z: an elaboration of methodology and findings. *Journal of Contemporary Business, 11*(2), 27-42.

Ouchi, William G. 1981. *Theory Z.* Reading, Mass.: Addison-Wesley.

Pagano, Clinton L., & Dintino, Justin J. 1982. Managing change: overhauling police management in a period of governmental retrenchment. *The Police Chief, 49,* 26-30.

Pauly, David, with Lubenow, Gerald C., & Reese, Michael. 1986, October 20. BankAmerica says 'no deal.' *Newsweek,* p. 56.

Peters, Charles. 1980. *How Washington Really Works.* Reading, Mass.: Addison-Wesley.

Peters, Thomas J., & Austin, Nancy. 1985, May 13. A passion for excellence. *Fortune,* pp. 20-32.

Peters, Thomas J., & Waterman, R. H., Jr. 1982. *In Search of Excellence.* New York: Harper & Row.

Platt, Harlan D. 1985. *Why Companies Fail.* Lexington, Mass.: D. C. Heath and Company.

Presidential Commission on the Space Shuttle Challenger Accident. June 6, 1986. *Report of the Presidential Commission on the Space Shuttle Challenger Accident,* Volume I. Washington, D.C.: Government Printing Office.

Questar, George H. 1984, August. Creativity and bureaucracy. *The Futurist, 18,* 27-29.

Quinn, James B. 1985, May-June. Managing innovation: controlled chaos. *Harvard Business Review,* pp. 73-84.

Ramaprasad, Arkalgud. 1982, October. Revolutionary change and strategic management. *Behavioral Science, 27,* 387-392.

Ramirez, Rafael. 1983. Action learning: a strategic approach for organizations facing turbulent conditions. *Human Relations, 36,* 725-742.

Randolph, Eleanor, & Behr, Peter. 1986, July 13. Newspaper preservation law produces windfalls. *Washington Post,* pp. A1, A11.

Rhodes, Lucien, with Amend, Patricia. 1986, August. The turnaround. *Inc.,* pp. 42-48.

Roggema, J., & Smith, M. H. 1983. Organizational change in the shipping industry: issues in the transformation of basic assumptions. *Human Relations, 36,* 765-790.

Rooney, James F. 1980. Organizational success through program failure: skid row rescue mission. *Social Forces, 58,* 904-924.

Rosenberg, Larry J., & Schewe, Charles D. 1985, July-August. Strategic planning: fulfilling the promise. *Business Horizons, 28*(4), 54-62.

Ruch, William V. 1984. *Corporate Communications.* Westport, Conn.: Quorum Books.

Sachs, Susan, & Cary, Peter. 1986, March 16. NASA is wasting millions, audits reveal. *Miami Herald,* p. 1.

Sanger, David E. 1986a, May 13. NASA had warning of risk to shuttle in cold weather. *New York Times,* p. 1.

Sanger, David E. 1986b, April 25. Shuttle photos: issue of crew's fate. *New York Times,* p. 11.

Sawyer, Kathy. 1988, January 26. More flaws found in space shuttle. *Washington Post,* p. A1.

Schmidt, Richard E., & Abramson, Mark A. 1983. Politics and performance: what does it mean for civil servants? *Public Administration Review, 43,* 155-165.

Scott, W. Richard. 1981. *Organizations: Rational, Natural, and Open Systems.* Englewood Cliffs, N.J.: Prentice-Hall, Inc.

Seeger, John A. 1984. Reversing the images of BCG's growth/share matrix. *Strategic Management Journal, 5,* 93-97.

Sherman, Stratford P. 1983, September 5. Muddling to victory at GEICO. *Fortune,* pp. 66-80.

Shifrin, Carole A. 1986, October 27. Texas Air officials named to fill top Eastern posts. *Aviation Week & Space Technology,* p. 34.

Sigafoos, Robert A. 1983. *Absolutely Positively Overnight!* Memphis, Tenn.: St. Luke's Press.

Singer, S. Fred. 1986, October 6. The case for going to Mars. *Newsweek,* p. 13.

Slevin, Dennis P., & Pinto, Jeffrey K. 1987. Balancing strategy and tactics in project implementation. *Sloan Management Review, 29*(1), 33-41.

Slote, Alfred. 1979. Termination at Baker Plant. In Kanter and Stein, pp. 412-428.

Smith, Bruce A. 1985, December 2. Propellant system tests will delay first Vandenberg Shuttle launch. *Aviation Week & Space Technology,* p. 20.

Smith, M. Elizabeth. 1982, December. Shrinking organizations: a management strategy for downsizing. *Business Quarterly,* pp. 30-33.

Spector, Bert. 1987. Transformational leadership: the new challenge for U.S. unions. *Human Resource Management, 26*(1), 3-16.

Stalker, Varena G. 1984. *A chronology of indigent care in Jefferson County.* Unpublished manuscript.

Starling, Grover. 1986. *Managing the Public Sector.* Chicago, Ill.: Dorsey Press.

Stavro, Barry. 1986. Digging out. *Forbes, 138*(10), 127-128.

Stein, Barry A. 1979. We're going to make sure this never happens again. In Kanter and Stein, pp. 394-399.

Steiss, Alan W. 1982. *Management Control in Government.* Lexington, Mass.: Lexington Books.

Stieglitz, Harold. 1985, April. The CEO today: a statesman's world view. *Across the Board,* pp. 47-52.

Sutton, Robert I. 1983. Managing organizational death. *Human Resource Management, 22*(4), 391-412.

Sutton, Robert I., Bruce, R. A., & Harris, S. G. 1983. Epilogue. *Human Resource Management, 22*(4), 467-473.

Swenson, Lloyd S., Jr., Grimwood, James S., & Alexander, Charles C. 1966. *This New Ocean.* Washington, D.C.: National Aeronautics and Space Administration.

Tainio, Risto, & Santalainen, Timo. 1984. Some evidence for the cultural relativity of organizational development programs. *Journal of Applied Behavioral Science, 20,* 93-111.

Tasini, Jonathan, with Bernstein, Aaron. 1987, March 30. Federal Express delivers a price shock. *Business Week,* p. 31-32.

Taylor, James C., & Asadorian, Robert A. 1985, July-August. The implementation of excellence: STS management. *Industrial Management, 27*(4), 5-15.

Thurow, Lester. 1984. Revitalizing American industry: managing in a competitive world economy. *California Management Review, 27*(1), 9-41.

Time. 1986, October 27. Back again, p. 74.

Time. 1985, October 21. Corporate identity crisis, p. 70.

Tjosvold, Dean. 1984. Effects of crisis orientation on managers' approach to controversy in decision making. *Academy of Management Journal, 27,* 130-138.

Toomey Company, Inc. 1984, June 29. *Assessment of the Management System and Services System of the South Carolina Department of Mental Health.* Greenville, S.C.: The Toomey Company.

Truskie, Stanley D. 1984, May-June. The driving force of successful organization. *Business Horizons,* pp. 43-48.

Tunstall, W. Brooke. 1983. Rites of passage. *Bell Telephone Magazine, 62*(3-4), Special Commemorative Edition, pp. 72-76.

United Press International. 1986a, October 11. BankAmerica Corp. chairman Samuel Armacost, resigns. *Birmingham Post-Herald,* p. A10.

United Press International. 1986b, August 12. USX cuts managers' pay 10%. *Birmingham Post-Herald,* p. B3.

U.S. Department of Education. 1984. *The Nation Responds: Recent Efforts to Improve Education.* Washington, D.C.: U.S. Government Printing Office.

U.S. News & World Report. 1982, August 9. How battered firms are surviving slump, pp. 29-30.

Usher, Cecil H. 1986. Culture in a squeeze: the impact of budget restrictions on organizational culture. Unpublished manuscript.

Vandervelde, Maryanne. 1981. Increasing people-productivity. *Journal of Contemporary Business, 10*(2), 19-32.

Vickery, Hugh B., III. 1983. It's the press. There's a crisis. What now? *Association Management, 35,* 47-51.

Walton, Richard E. 1985, March-April. From control to commitment in the workplace. *Harvard Business Review,* pp. 77-84.

Weir, David. 1975. Stress and the manager in the over-controlled organization. In Dan Gowler & Karen Legge (Eds.), *Managerial Stress,* 165-178. New York: John Wiley & Sons.

Werther, William B., Jr. 1982. Quality Circles: key executive issues. *Journal of Contemporary Business, 11*(2), 17-26.

Whetten, D. A. 1980. Organizational decline: a neglected topic in organizational science. *Academy of Management Review, 5,* 577-588.

Willie Wilson, Jr., et al. v. State of Alabama, No.: CV83-PT-2866-S, unpublished op. (D.Ala. April 11, 1985).

Zammuto, Raymond F. 1985. Managing decline: lessons from the U.S. auto industry. *Administration & Society, 17*(1), 71-95.

Index

ABOUT THE AUTHOR

MARY E. GUY is Associate Professor of Political Science and Public Affairs at the University of Alabama at Birmingham. Her research interests focus on behavior in organizations, and she teaches in the graduate program in public administration. Before joining the UAB faculty in 1982, Dr. Guy worked for the South Carolina Department of Mental Health and the Georgia Department of Human Resources.

Dr. Guy's writings target the topics of conflict in organizations, team building, communication flows, and program evaluation. She is author of *Professionals in Organizations: Debunking a Myth* as well as many articles. Her research has appeared in numerous journals, including *Group and Organization Studies, Hospital and Health Services Administration, Administration in Mental Health, Dimensions of Critical Care Nursing,* and *New England Journal of Human Services.*